vessels,
vehicles,
and
victory

vessels, vehicles, and victory

UNFORGETTABLE MEN OF THE BIBLE

j. vernon mc gee

MOODY PRESS

CHICAGO

Moody Press Combined Edition

© 1976 by
THE MOODY BIBLE INSTITUTE
OF CHICAGO

Second Printing, 1976

Library of Congress Cataloging in Publication Data

McGee, John Vernon, 1904-
    Vessels, vehicles, and victory.

    1. Bible—Biography. I. Title.

BS571.M253   220.9'2 [B]   76-9042

ISBN 0-8024-9157-X

Printed in the United States of America

CONTENTS

1

WHY THE FLOOD?

Noah

Genesis 6-7

When rains come to Southern California, the metro-
politan newspapers carry headlines: FLOOD DISASTER.
It sounds like Noah's day, and for those who live in the
flooded areas, it does mean disaster. But for Southern
California generally, the rains are worth millions of dollars
and are a great blessing.

By the same token, the Flood of Noah's day was a judgment from God upon mankind, but it was also a blessing
in disguise. And God's mercy was manifested in the Flood
that came.

Some Christian geologists treat the Flood of Noah's day
as one in a series of local catastrophes, and they attach no
particular significance to the Flood recorded in Genesis 7,
other than it was probably the last in this series. They do
not deny the Flood; they merely attempt to relegate it to
a place of unimportance.

However, there has been a return to the old theory that
the Flood is the explanation for the geological formations
that are found all over the world today. Let me share with
you an excerpt from the book, *The Genesis Flood*, written
by Henry Morris and John C. Whitcomb.

> Throughout the eighteenth century, and well into the
> nineteenth, most theologians and scientists of the west-

7

ern world believed that the Deluge was responsible for
the major fossiliferous strata of the earth. But the rise
of Cuvier's theory of successive catastrophes, which as-
signed most of the fossil strata to ages long before the
creation of man, caused many to abandon the older
Flood theory of geology. William Buckland led the way
in Great Britain by pointing to "diluvium" deposits as
positive evidence of the last and greatest catastrophe in
the history of the earth—the Genesis Flood.

But no sooner had a large number of Christians accepted the "successive catastrophes" view than Buckland
and Sedgwick, along with other geologists, began to make
public recantations of their former views. The "diluvium" deposits were no longer attributed to the Flood,
but to the last of a series of pre-Adamic catastrophes.
The Flood, though still regarded as universal, was now
depicted as a comparatively "tranquil" affair, which
left no discernible geologic effects.

By now, the Church was ready for the final stage of
the harmonization process; for in 1839 John Pye Smith
set forth his theory that the Flood was nothing but a
local inundation in the Mesopotamian Valley. Freed at
long last from the necessity of harmonizing geology with
Genesis, scientists dismissed the Genesis Flood from
their minds and joined Sir Charles Lyell in his efforts to
"patiently untie the Gordian knot" of fossiliferous strata
according to the uniformitarian principles which he had
enunciated as early as 1830.[1]

At the conclusion of the book, they give the "Bankruptcy
of Uniformitarianism" because it never really explained
anything.

The present widely accepted system of uniformitarianism in historical geology, with its evolutionary basis and
bias, has been shown to be utterly inadequate to explain
most of the important geologic phenomena. Present
rates and processes simply *cannot* account for the great
bulk of geological data. Some form of catastrophism is

1. John C. Whitcomb, Jr., and Henry M. Morris, *The Genesis Flood*
(Philadelphia: Presby. & Reformed, 1968), pp. 113-14.

clearly indicated by the vast evidences of volcanism, diastrophism, glaciation, coal and oil and mineral deposits, fossilization, vast beds of sediments, and most of the other dominant features of the earth's crust. When this fact is once recognized, it can then be seen that even the supposed evidences of great geologic age can be reinterpreted to correlate well with the much more impelling evidences of violent and rapid activity and formation.[2]

So that today there is a move back to the old position, and men of real intellectual stature and scientific background are taking that position today. This is important.

The Flood, therefore, was global in extent; it was devastating in its effect and permanent in geological evidence that it left.

The record given to us by Moses in Genesis is actually a restrained account. It is not extreme nor extravagant. There is no labored elaboration of detail and absolutely no excess verbiage at all in the record that has been given to us.

For instance, notice what is said concerning the ark: "And this is the fashion which thou shalt make it of: The length of the ark shall be three hundred cubits, the breadth of it fifty cubits, and the height of it thirty cubits" (Gen 6:15).

The size of the ark is quite interesting. It is not the ridiculous little boat pictured on Sunday school literature. If you will examine the measurements here, you will find that they are about six to one; that is, the width of it is about one-sixth of the length of it. If you will put that down by the measurements of the battleship *New Mexico* that a few years ago was considered the finest example of modern engineering (it was 624 feet long, 106¼ feet wide, and 29½ feet the mean draft), you will find that the ark measurements are the same in ratio. If you imagine the ark to be some sort of crude structure, you apparently are

2. Ibid., p. 439.

not acquainted with the information given in the Word of God.

"A window shalt thou make to the ark, and in a cubit shalt thou finish it above; and the door of the ark shalt thou set in the side thereof; with lower, second, and third stories shalt thou make it" (Gen 6:16). The window in the ark was not a little cubbyhole cut in the side of the ark, as pictured on my Sunday school card, but was probably a window one cubit from the top that went all the way around the ark. Modern gymnasiums today have that kind of ventilation.

Also it had three decks—"with lower, second, and third stories shalt thou make it." The ark was by no means the crude structure it is sometimes made out to be.

Also there are those who ridicule the story by characterizing Noah as sort of a "Bring 'em back alive" Frank Buck. Noah was not a big game hunter; I don't believe he went out after the animals. More likely the animals came to him.

A ranger at Yosemite was telling me that when the snow is gone from the top of the mountain, you can't get within eyesight or earshot, certainly not within gunshot, of the deer. But when the snows begin to fall and bury the vegetation, those little deer will come down and eat out of your hand. Animals will come to man in time of danger. The animals at the time of the Flood came to Noah—that is what is said here: "Of fowls after their kind, and of cattle after their kind, of every creeping thing of the earth after his kind, two of every sort shall come unto thee, to keep them alive. . . . There went in two and two unto Noah into the ark, the male and the female, as God had commanded Noah" (Gen 6:20; 7:9).

Noah's problem, I imagine, was not to get in the required number but to keep out the others. I have wondered how he managed to limit the number of each kind.

The ark itself and the account of the Flood carries a great deal of geological and historical evidence, and is a fascinating subject for research and exploration. However, it is not my intention to deal with this aspect of the Flood. Rather, I want to deal with this question: Why the Flood? Why did God send the flood? Why was this type of extreme surgery needed on the human race? There are those who are saying today that capital punishment is not humane. Believe me, God had mass execution in this day. Why was it necessary? Why the Flood?

"And it came to pass, when men began to multiply on the face of the earth, and daughters were born unto them, that the sons of God saw the daughters of men that they were fair; and they took them wives of all which they chose" (Gen 6:1-2). Many fine expositors give to this text a rather unnatural interpretation. They say that the sons of God were angels, that the daughters of men were human beings, and that this is the intermarriage of supernatural creatures with mankind. Now I personally cannot accept this interpretation because I do not think such a union could exist. Our Lord definitely said that angels neither marry nor are given in marriage (Mt 22:30), and I would take it that this would be entirely out of keeping with the purpose for which they were created. They were never told to multiply as man was told to multiply. Each was a separate creation of itself. Also we must assume that good angels would not commit this sin; and bad angels could never be called the "sons of God." Also the offspring were men, not monsters. "But," some folks say, "it says that their offspring were giants." It does not.

"There were giants in the earth in those days; and also after that, when the sons of God came in unto the daughters of men, and they bare children to them, the same became mighty men which were of old, men of renown" (Gen 6:4). Notice that there were giants in the earth *before* this intermingling took place. Giants were not the result of it. However giants did exist. They were the result of the offspring of Adam.

To rightly interpret this verse we must keep in mind the

theme of Genesis. Moses, writing under inspiration, is not trying to tell us about creation or about the Flood. Rather, he is tracing the families, and one family in particular that is going to lead to Jesus Christ. Genesis is the record of the family tree from the first man, Adam. There is a line that leads all the way through the Old Testament to the Lord Jesus Christ. If you consult the two genealogies (Mt 1:1-16 and Lk 3:23-28), you will see that the two genealogies go right back into the book of Genesis; they are grounded there. That is the thing that lends importance to the book of Genesis.

There is a definite pattern that is followed in the book of Genesis. God will give a rejected line first and then dismiss it. Then God takes the chosen line (which will lead to Christ) and pushes it on through. For instance, Abraham had two sons, Ishmael and Isaac. Ishmael's line is given to us and then is dismissed. Then the line of Isaac is given and is pursued all the way through the Bible so that the New Testament opens with the fact that Jesus Christ is a son of Isaac, which is the reason that line is followed.

Now, going back to the fourth chapter of Genesis, we see Cain's line. "And Cain went out from the presence of the LORD, and dwelt in the land of Nod, on the east of Eden" (Gen 4:16). Then the line of Cain is given, but it is not followed through.

In chapter five the line of Seth is given. Noah is in this line, and his is the one that is followed. Chapter six states the simple fact that the godly line that came from Seth is now intermarried with the ungodly line of Cain. The sons of God (this godly line) chose wives on the basis of physical beauty: they "saw the daughters of men that they were fair"; they had no regard for the spiritual side at all. You will see the intermarrying of these two, the godly with the ungodly, all the way through the Scriptures. The most notable example, I guess, is Ahab, king of God's people Israel, and Jezebel, daughter of Ethbaal, priest of the most pagan religion in the world. This marriage had a disastrous effect on the entire nation.

Also in our day the intermarriage of believers and unbelievers is a most dangerous thing. God records it here before the Flood as a warning to us today.

The day came, therefore, when only one man among the millions on this earth found grace in the eyes of the Lord. "But Noah found grace in the eyes of the LORD" (Gen 6:8). Because of the intermarriage and the intrusion of that which was godless into the godly line, men and women were produced who turned their back on God. Finally we get down to where there was one who did not— *one!* How tragic! The cancer of sin was terminal. The human race was suffering from the incurable disease of sin. And no one would turn to God in the next generation. The entire human family would be lost. Therefore God moved in while He had only one man left. God was long-suffering; He was patient; He saw this erosion of spiritual life, man turning away from Him; He waited until there was only one man left. If He had waited any longer the entire race would have been lost.

May I say to you, friend, the Flood was a judgment, an awful judgment. God never said it wasn't awful; it was awful. But it *was* a blessing in disguise. The reason today that you and I have been able to hear the Gospel and be saved is that God brought His judgment of the Flood when He did. He waited as long as He could. Only Noah was left. Only one turned to God. This is shocking, I admit. Only *one!*

"These are the generations of Noah: Noah was a just man and perfect in his generations, and Noah walked with God" (Gen 6:9). When it says that Noah was perfect and walked with God, it means that he did what Enoch did, what Abel did: those who were God's men had been beating a path to an altar. And I can see Noah taking his little sacrifice, his little lamb, and heading for that altar. The grass had grown up around it because men were no longer

going there; they were going their own way. But here is a
man who walked with God, and when he walked with God
he walked to that altar. This means that he acknowledged
that he was a sinner and needed a Saviour. When he did
that, he was made acceptable to Almighty God. It was
God's way for man to go.

THE EARTH IN DISGRACE

"And God looked upon the earth, and, behold, it was
corrupt; for all flesh had corrupted his way upon the
earth" (Gen 6:12). What does it mean by "his way upon
the earth"? Whose way? Well, it means simply this: it
was man's way, but it was the way that God had marked
out for him. It was to that altar that man could repair,
acknowledge that he was a sinner, and on the basis of that,
offer a sacrifice that made him righteous before God. That
is God's way, not man's way. But man had corrupted his
way upon the earth.

Because he did not come God's way, notice the condition
of man in that day. This is the fruit of sin: "And God saw
that the wickedness of man was great in the earth, and
that every imagination of the thoughts of his heart was
only evil continually" (Gen 6:5). Notice the pyramiding
of modifiers here. The wickedness of man was *great* in the
earth (his wickedness was not little, and not just some of
his imagination and thoughts were evil occasionally).
Every imagination and thought was *only* evil *continually!*
This is the picture of mankind. Someone has said that
the heart is the thought factory of man. The Lord Jesus
said, "Out of the heart proceed the issues of life." The
heart refers to our inmost being, where we live and move
and have our being.

I wonder if you have noted this prayer of David: "O
LORD God of Abraham, Isaac, and of Israel, our fathers,
keep this for ever in the imagination of the thoughts of the
heart of thy people, and prepare their heart unto thee"
(1 Ch 29:18).

This was his prayer when he dedicated the place where the Temple was to be built, a place where God's people could come and have their thoughts and imaginations drawn to Him. But here in Noah's day, folk had left God out of their lives entirely. They no longer went to the altar. But the thoughts and the imaginations of their heart was only evil—evil continually.

Now primarily, what was their sin? Can we specifically label it? I think we can. The words of our Lord shed light upon their sin. "And as it was in the days of Noe, so shall it be also in the days of the Son of man. They did eat, they drank, they married wives, they were given in marriage, until the day that Noe entered into the ark, and the flood came, and destroyed them all" (Lk 17:26-27).

A great many authors and speakers attempt to depict the days of Noah. They do not get their information from the Bible, although, of course, an inference can be drawn from what is recorded. However, the Word of God is specific. Our Lord said that in the days of Noah they were eating and drinking. Is that wrong? No, it is not. Then what did our Lord mean? Also He said that they were marrying and giving in marriage. That's all right. Isn't it? Certainly. Then what was the sin? Well, when you go back and read the passage, the thing that was wrong was that they just left God out. They were eating and drinking as though God did not exist. Noah said a flood was coming; they ridiculed him and lived as if nothing in the world was going to happen. They paid no attention to God; they had no relationship with Him; they lived as if God did not exist. That is the thing that is wrong. They just left Him out of their lives.

Let me make this statement: I am more and more coming to the conviction that the worst sin is unbelief. No sin compares to the sin of unbelief. It is the most deadly virus known to man. You and I cannot conceive of the extent of this awful thing known as unbelief—just leaving God out. You remember that the Lord Jesus Himself said, "It is expedient for you that I go away; for if I go not away, the Comforter will not come unto you; but if I depart, I will send him unto you. And when he is come, he will reprove the world of sin, and of righteousness, and of judgment: of sin [What sin? Murder? No.] because they believe not on me" (Jn 16:7-9). This is the big sin today. If you are an unbeliever, my friend, the difficulty and problem is not some great sin you might have committed, or some mental hurdle you have to get over; your problem is a heart of unbelief. And that is the most vile, wicked thing there is in God's sight. Do you know how practical this is? Let me give you an example.

The United States Republic is based upon these principles:

1. There is a God.
2. Individuals have rights derived from God.
3. There is self-government to protect those rights.

International Communism, based upon the theories and writings of Karl Marx, Lenin and Stalin, has the following postulates:

1. There is no God.
2. Men have no rights.
3. The State is All.
4. There is no Truth.

Now, friend, they tell me that Communism is something new. It is as old as the Flood. The problem in the days of Noah was that they said, "There is no God." You can call it by any label you choose, but, my beloved, that is what brought the Flood! And America today is as far from God as Russia is far from God. Oh, I don't say that America is Communistic, but we are *agnostic*. Rightist movements can be, and some of them are, as far from God as any of the leftist movements. We have become a godless nation. The sex revolution, the marching and protesting and rioting, are fruit of the awful unbelief that has come into this country which was founded on the fact that there is a God. Even preachers have turned away from the Word of God. You and I are living in alarming days. The days of the Flood have returned. Unbelief was their sin.

Noah was a preacher of righteousness. What kind of righteousness did he preach? The righteousness that a man got when he went to that altar with his animal sacrifice, recognizing that he was a sinner, and that a penalty had to be paid for his sin. Noah preached that kind of righteousness.

This is what Peter means in 1 Peter 3:18-20: "For Christ also hath once suffered for sins, the just for the unjust, that he might bring us to God." That is the reason Christ died. That altar to which Noah went pointed to Him. "Being put to death in the flesh but made alive by the Spirit, by whom also he went and preached unto the spirits in prison" (NSRB*). When did Christ do that? I hear the foolish interpretation that Christ after His crucifixion went down in the lower regions and preached. Why would He do that? They had no second chance. Then when did He preach to them? Peter tells us: "Who at one time were disobedient, when once the longsuffering of God waited in the days of Noah, while the ark was preparing, in which few, that is, eight souls, were saved by water" (NSRB). When Noah preached, Christ was preaching through him. Noah presented a Saviour to the world of his day. This preaching took place back in the days of Noah. Christ preached through Noah for one hundred and twenty years.

"And the LORD said, My Spirit shall not always strive with man, for that he also is flesh: yet his days shall be an hundred and twenty years" (Gen 6:3). For one hundred twenty years God was patient, God was waiting.

For one hundred twenty years Noah was a witness: "By faith Noah, being warned of God of things not seen as yet, moved with fear, prepared an ark to the saving of

*New Scofield Reference Bible

his house; by the which he condemned the world, and became heir of the righteousness which is by faith" (Heb 11:7). This man was a witness to his world that he believed God.

Leaving God out led, of course, to loose living and no regard for others. This follows: "The earth also was corrupt before God, and the earth was filled with violence. And God looked upon the earth, and behold, it was corrupt; for all flesh had corrupted his way upon the earth. And God said unto Noah, The end of all flesh is come before me; for the earth is filled with violence through them; and, behold, I will destroy them with the earth" (Gen 6:11-13). The earth here begins to get the results of this business of unbelief.

Believe me, America today is feeling the violence that is coming through lawlessness. You do not pick up a newspaper without reading about lawlessness—violence everywhere. And they are trying to doctor the symptoms. Actually violence is the symptom of this awful disease of unbelief that has come to our nation.

That is exactly what our Lord said, even in the Sermon on the Mount, which liberals love to quote. They say that they live by the Golden Rule; then let's see them follow through on it: "Therefore all things whatever ye would that men should do to you, do ye even so to them: for this is the law and the prophets" (Mt 7:12).

"Let your light so shine before men, that they may see your good works, and glorify your Father, which is in heaven" (Mt 5:16). The Sermon on the Mount is theocentric (not anthropocentric, as one liberal said); it is God-centered. Man must be rightly related to God, and man's conduct must be in obedience to the revelation of God. If it is not, then that man is a lawless man!

There is a message for us here in 2 Peter 3:1-6: "This second epistle, beloved, I now write unto you; in both which I stir up your pure minds by way of remembrance: that ye may be mindful of the words which were spoken before by the holy prophets, and of the commandment of us, the apostles of the Lord and Saviour; knowing this first, that there shall come in the last days scoffers, walking after their own lusts." The "scoffers, walking after their own lusts" are here; they are abroad in the land. If you are a Christian I hope you have found out that you are in a minority group—really a minority group. The scoffers are the majority. But as long as I can lift my voice, I want to make it very clear that the hope of the world is the coming of Christ. His return is being denied everywhere. "And saying, Where is the promise of his coming? for since the fathers fell asleep, all things continue as they were from the beginning of the creation." The curse of the hour is the skepticism. "Where is the promise of His coming?" "For this they willingly are ignorant of, that by the word of God the heavens were of old, and the earth standing out of the water and in the water." They deny that the Flood took place; but God says it did. "Whereby the world that then was, being overflowered with water, perished."

It is said that judgment has gone out of style and that there is not a preacher of any stature or intelligence that would dare preach judgment today! However, there are men of both intelligence and stature who are preaching judgment. Paul, the greatest preacher of them all, did: "And after certain days, when Felix came with his wife, Drusilla, who was a Jewess, he sent for Paul, and heard him concerning the faith in Christ. And as he reasoned of righteousness, self-control, and judgment to come, Felix trembled, and answered, Go thy way for this time; when I have a convenient season, I will call for thee" (Ac 24:24-25, NSRB). This man Felix did not want to hear any more. He didn't want to hear about judgment to come.

Our Lord said in Luke 18:8, "When the Son of Man cometh, shall he find faith on the earth?" *Faith* is an abstract term. Everybody has faith in something. But the "faith" our Lord speaks of here is the body of revealed

truth. Will He find that when He returns? The way the
question is couched in the Greek, it demands a negative
answer. The answer is no.

Why hasn't judgment already come? "The Lord is not
slack concerning his promise, as some men count slack-
ness; but is longsuffering to us, not willing that any should
perish, but that all should come to repentance" (2 Pe 3:9,
NSRB).

Before the days of Noah there was the warning. The
birth of Methuselah was a warning. The name "Methuselah" means *he has sent his death,* and the year that
Methuselah died the Flood came. Yet God prolonged his
life for 969 years. God said it was coming; it had to come
for the sake of the generations that were yet to be born
on the earth. He had to do it. It was an act of mercy for
them. For one hundred twenty years God warned them
through the preaching of Noah. "It's coming!" The people
laughed, "All things continue as they were. You must
have missed it, Brother Noah. The weather report is fair
and warmer!" Noah said, "It is coming."

"By faith Noah, being warned of God of things not seen
as yet, moved with fear, prepared an ark to the saving of
his house" (Heb 11:7). There wasn't a cloud in the sky.
They hadn't even had a good *fog,* but Noah persisted, "It's
coming." One hundred twenty years went by, and then it
came.

You and I live in a day when men insist that we have
moved out of the orbit of judgment and the idea of a God
that judges. In fact, they have concluded that we don't
even need God, that things will continue as they are.

Frankly, I'd like to rush Him. Oh, if I could get a tele-
gram to Him, I'd tell Him to hurry. But He is not hurry-
ing. He has eternity ahead of Him. Someone asks, "Do
you think judgment will come in our lifetime?" I don't
know. He has told us only that it is coming, and for you
it won't be long, because you will not be here very much
longer. Time is against you.

You are having your opportunity now to decide for or against Christ. And I believe, frankly, that the ministry should be sharpened down to one point: declare the Word of God. That's all. Let the chips fall where they may. "But," someone argues, "I know a very brilliant man, and he doesn't believe the Bible." I'm not worried about him at all. What he thinks makes no difference. It was pretty hard in Noah's time to have the world against you, but it sure was nice to be right the day the Flood came.

Dwight L. Moody said this:

> I look upon this world as a wrecked vessel. Its ruin is getting nearer and nearer. God said to me, "Moody, here is a lifeboat. Go out and rescue as many as you can before the crash comes." The churches are asleep. I know of no better way to awaken them than to get them to look for the return of their Lord from heaven. Nowhere in the Scriptures is it claimed that the whole world will be brought to the feet of Christ in this dispensation. I do not find any place in the Bible where God says that the world is to grow better and better and that Christ is to have a spiritual reign over the earth a thousand years. The first thing Christ is to do at His coming is to take the Church out of the world. The trump of God may be sounded before anything we do—before I have finished this address.

However, that was years ago, and still Christ has not come. Do you know why Christ has not come before this? It is not because He is not coming; it is because He is long-suffering and patient. He is not willing that any should perish. He has tomorrow, and tomorrow, and tomorrow.

But you don't!

2

BACK TO BETHEL

Jacob

Genesis 27-35

The geographical location of Bethel is about twelve miles north of Jerusalem. It is described as a bleak moorland in the hill country. It stands twelve hundred feet above sea level, where the wild winds whistle about its large exposed rocks. If you have driven over the old dirt roads between California's Yucca Valley and Apple Valley, you have seen a place much like Bethel. Although the topography was desolate and forbidding, it was the spiritual high point in the life of Jacob.

To understand the Scripture before us, we must go back thirty years to the time when Jacob first went to Bethel. At that time, he was fleeing for his life. His brother, Esau, was after him to murder him. Jacob was a fugitive, a runaway. He had no traveling gear whatsoever except a staff in his hand. That first night away from home he spent at Bethel, his head pillowed on a stone in that bleak, lonely spot, with the winds howling about him. He dreamed of a ladder that was set up on earth; the top of it reached to heaven, and God stood above that ladder.

What was it that brought him to this place? What kind of a home did he leave? It was not an ideal home, but it was a home through which God was moving for time and for eternity. It was the home of Isaac and Rebekah.

Isaac was the son of Abraham and Sarah, the son of promise. God had given him to them in their old age by miracle. When the boy was grown, his old father refused to take a wife for him from among the heathen in whose land they lived. He instructed his servant to get a bride for his son from among his kinfolk back at Haran. The servant, unerringly guided by God, brought back Rebekah to be the bride of Isaac. We take up the thread of their story when they were expecting their first child.

"And the children struggled together within her; and she said, If it be so, why am I thus? And she went to inquire of the LORD. And the LORD said unto her, Two nations are in thy womb, and two manner of people shall be separated from thy bowels; and the one people shall be stronger than the other people; and the elder shall serve the younger" (Gen 25:22-23).

God said that two nations were to come out of this family, and two nations did come from these two boys. We shall follow them through the Word of God.

Not only can we trace the history of these two nations, but we are given the spiritual application to the life of the believer. You see, all truth in the Bible is germinative in Genesis. We find the seed plot of the Bible in the book of Genesis, and we have the bud appearing there; much of the Bible is simply the unfolding. In Esau and Jacob we have a picture of the two natures in a believer today. If you are a child of God, you have a new nature, but you did not get rid of your old nature, and because of this there is conflict. The new nature and the old nature are opposed to each other. Paul said that the flesh wars against the Spirit, and the Spirit wars against the flesh. Esau pictures the flesh, Jacob the spirit.

Esau, the man of the flesh, was outwardly far more attractive than Jacob. He was an outdoor man, the athletic type. He was the popular man, the extrovert, the man of the world. In contrast, Jacob was the man of the spirit— although that is not apparent at the beginning. When we

first meet him he is actually much less attractive than
Esau. He is clever, self-opinionated, crooked as can be,
and above all, he is mamma's boy.

"And Isaac loved Esau, because he did eat of his venison:
but Rebekah loved Jacob" (Gen 25:28). In this family
both parents have their favorites, which invariably creates
friction. As these boys are growing up, you will notice
that they are not identical twins; rather they are oppo-
sites. God said before they were born—so it would be of
grace—"I have chosen the younger, and the elder will
serve him." Jacob, knowing God's promise, still connived
for the right of the firstborn.

The birthright may not seem very important to you, but
it actually meant that the boy possessing it would be the
priest of the family, and it guaranteed that the promise
made to the father would be confirmed to him. The ulti-
mate promise was that the Messiah would come through
the line of the one having the birthright. Esau, a man of
the flesh, did not care about what might happen a thousand
years from his day. He was unconcerned about anything
beyond his present life. His philosophy was eat, drink,
and be merry, for tomorrow we die.

Esau came in from hunting, hungry—but not starving
to death. Jacob did not take advantage of a starving man.
Do you think anyone could have starved to death in the
wealthy home of Abraham or Isaac? Of course not. But
when he smelled the aroma of his brother's cooking, he
wanted it. Now, you get nothing from Jacob unless you
pay for it, and Jacob bargained, "I'll let you have it if you
will let me have that birthright you don't care about."
Esau so despised his birthright that he said, "You may
have it; it means nothing to me." Thus Jacob bought that
which God had already promised to give him; he had to
get it on his own. God could not, nor did He, approve this
transaction.

Jacob did not stop there. When old Isaac was about to
do that which he should not have done—bless Esau—

Jacob and his mother schemed. Actually they stole the blessing. Isaac had said to Esau, "And make me savoury meat, such as I love, and bring it to me, that I may eat; that my soul may bless thee before I die" (Gen 27:4).

Rebekah and Jacob collaborated in the deception: "And Rebekah took goodly raiment of her eldest son Esau, which were with her in the house, and put them upon Jacob her younger son: and she put the skins of the kids of the goats upon his hands, and upon the smooth of his neck: and she gave the savoury meat and the bread, which she had prepared, into the hand of her son Jacob. And he came unto his father, and said, My father: and he said, Here am I; who art thou, my son? And Jacob said unto his father, I am Esau thy firstborn; I have done according as thou badest me: arise, I pray thee, sit and eat of my venison, that thy soul may bless me" (Gen 27:15-19).

Isaac, his senses dimmed by age, was taken in by the clever ruse. "And he came near, and kissed him: and he smelled the smell of his raiment, and blessed him, and said, See, the smell of my son is as the smell of a field which the LORD hath blessed: therefore God give thee the dew of heaven, and the fatness of the earth, and plenty of corn and wine: let people serve thee, and nations bow down to thee: be lord over thy brethren, and let thy mother's sons bow down to thee: cursed be every one that curseth thee, and blessed be he that blesseth thee" (Gen 27:27-29).

The theft of the blessing was the straw that broke the camel's back; it turned his brother against him. "And Esau hated Jacob because of the blessing wherewith his father blessed him: and Esau said in his heart, The days of mourning for my father are at hand; then will I slay my brother Jacob" (Gen 27:41). *My father is old,* he thought, *and I don't want to do anything that would put him in his grave; but the minute he dies, I am going to kill my brother.*

Now then Rebekah hears about this threat to her favorite son, she says to Jacob, "Now therefore, my son,

obey my voice; and arise, flee thou to Laban my brother to
Haran; and tarry with him a few days, until thy brother's
fury turn away" (Gen 27:43-44). She told him to go for
just a few days, but the days lengthened into thirty years,
and in the meantime Rebekah died. She never saw her
boy again. Her sin was judged.

This old boy leaves home and spends his first night out
at Bethel. That night he dreams of a ladder set up on
earth with angels upon it. If I had written this account,
I would have said that the angels come from heaven, descending; and then return, ascending. But the record does
not read that way. It states that the angels were ascending
and descending. What does that mean? God is telling
Jacob that He would answer prayer. The ascending angel,
the prayer; the descending angel, the answer, and the ladder is our Lord Jesus Christ.

In the New Testament, when Jesus called Nathanael,
He characterized him as an Israelite in whom was no guile,
no *Jacob*—none of his cleverness, none of his crookedness,
none of his self-opinionatedness. Nathanael was a sincere
man who had questioned the Messiahship of Jesus. "Can
any good thing come out of Nazareth?" he had wisecracked
to Philip. But Jesus said to him, "Before that Philip called
thee, when thou wast under the fig tree, I saw thee. Nathanael answered and saith unto him, Rabbi, thou art the
Son of God; thou art the King of Israel. Jesus answered
and said unto him, Because I said unto thee, I saw thee
under the fig tree, believest thou? thou shalt see greater
things than these. And he saith unto him, Verily, verily,
I say unto you, Hereafter ye shall see heaven open, and
the angels of God ascending and descending upon the Son
of Man" (Jn 1:48-51).

Christ is the ladder; and, when Jacob pillowed his head
on the stones at Bethel with the wild winds racing about
him, he dreamed of that ladder. He had thought he had
left God back home. Listen to him: "And Jacob awaked
out of his sleep, and he said, Surely the LORD is in this

place; and I knew it not" (Gen 28:16). You see, though down deep Jacob had a spiritual nature, he had connived and schemed, depending on his own wits and his own strength. He was far from God. This man, when he left home and escaped from Esau, mopped his brow and said, "Good-bye, Esau, Good-bye, God." He honestly thought he had left God back home, but the first night out God appeared to him. He was telling this lonesome, homesick boy that there is grace and mercy with God, that he still had access to God; his prayers would be heard and his prayers would be answered. God had not forsaken him.

In chapter 10 of Romans where Paul discusses the nation Israel and especially this Jacob and his brother, Esau, he goes on, in verses 6-8, to say something that is quite interesting: "But the righteousness which is of faith speaketh on this wise, Say not in thine heart, Who shall ascend into heaven? (that is, to bring Christ down from above:)." You do not have to bring Christ down a ladder today. He is available to you—right where you are sitting. "Or, who shall descend into the deep? (that is, to bring up Christ again from the dead.)" He is already back from the dead, my beloved. "But what saith it? The word is nigh thee, even in thy mouth, and in thy heart: that is, the word of faith, which we preach."

Such is the Gospel which we preach today, the Gospel of a ladder reaching to heaven. God is available. You do not have to go through a religious system, a church, or a preacher. There is nothing (this is the frightening thing, and it is the thing that frightened Jacob) between your soul and God. When you are running away from your brother because you have deceived him, when you are out of the will of God, such a discovery is frightening. God says to you and He says to me, "There is not even a tissue between your soul and me. I am available." The Lord Jesus says, "I am the ladder." "If thou shalt confess with thy mouth the Lord Jesus, and shalt believe in thine heart that God hath raised him from the dead, thou shalt be saved. For with the heart man believeth unto righteousness; and with the mouth confession is made unto salvation" (Ro 10:9-10).

There is a ladder let down from heaven right where you are at this moment, so that all you have to do is bring your mouth and your heart into harmony—so that they say the same thing. Trust Christ as your personal Saviour today, and believe that God gave Him for your sin and that God raised Him from the dead, and you shall be saved. The way is wide open for you today. No man is able to open it, but Christ opened it for you over nineteen hundred years ago. Christ is the ladder.

Jacob found that ladder when he ran away from home. And God promised to be with him. Imagine God promising to be with this clever, self-opinionated old boy who thinks he knows everything! "Behold, I am with thee, and will keep thee in all places whither thou goest, and will bring thee again into this land; for I will not leave thee, until I have done that which I have spoken to thee of" (Gen 28:15). God says, "I will not leave you, I will not forsake you. You did not run away from Me. I am going to continue to deal with you." Believe me, God dealt with this boy—which we shall see.

Notice the reaction of this runaway! I told you he was frightened. "He was afraid, and said, How dreadful is this place!"

You know, that is the reason some folk will not come to Bible study. They have a hundred excuses, but the real reason is they do not want to get that close to God. Actually the reason multitudes of folk want to go through a ceremony, a ritual, a church, or a man, is so that they will not have to go firsthand to God. But nineteen hundred years ago, He cut out the middleman and you go to Him *directly*.

Listen to Jacob: "How dreadful is this place! this is none other but the house of God, and this is the gate of heaven" (Gen 28:17). This is Bethel. Such was his experience, and now he makes his vow.

"And Jacob vowed a vow, saying, If God will be with me, and will keep me in this way that I go, and will give me bread to eat, and raiment to put on, so that I come again to my father's house in peace; then shall the LORD be my God" (Gen 28:20-21).

He couldn't help but trade! Even after God promised to do it for him, he turned right around and said, *"If God will do this for me, then He will be my God"*—always trading, always depending on himself to work something out. However, this experience at Bethel is the high point in his life. I believe it is his conversion.

On to Haran now, on to the place where his mother had sent him—to her brother's home. Jacob resumed his journey, cocksure, self-sufficient, conceited. However, unbeknown to him, he was moving toward college—the college of hard knocks. His uncle Laban was dean and professor of all the courses. And, believe me, he was a good teacher.

When Jacob arrived in Haran, he met a girl. She was Rachel. She came to the well with her father's sheep. Jacob watered the sheep, then (I always have been amused at this) he kissed Rachel, and lifted up his voice and wept. It was love at first sight. She was the only fine thing in this man's life. She was at his side through all the hard years in Haran. After many years they had a son, Joseph. Later Benjamin was born at Bethlehem. His birth cost Rachel's life, and it was at Bethlehem that Jacob buried his beautiful Rachel.

But now Jacob had just arrived at Haran and had met Rachel. She led him to her home because she was the daughter of Uncle Laban. Jacob didn't know it, but he was in school now. Here he was, the nephew who had come from a far country. But he was a guest for only a few days. He expected to be treated in style. He had been able to outwit everybody, including his father and his brother; but he had encountered Uncle Laban now, and Uncle Laban was smarter than he was.

One morning at breakfast Uncle Laban said, "Because thou art my brother, shouldest thou therefore serve me for nought? tell me, what shall thy wages be?" "You're my brother. I'm not going to let you work here for nothing." Who said anything about *working?* Jacob had not. He had not come to Haran to work. That boy lived, not by the sweat of his brow and the hands of toil, but by his wits. Yet here somebody was getting in ahead of him. Uncle Laban said, "I'm not going to let you work for nothing, but tomorrow morning you're getting up with the other hired help and you are going to start working for me—and I'll pay you."

Now he had already seen Jacob mooning at Rachel. He knew what Jacob wanted, and he knew what he intended to give him. Jacob fell right into line: "I will serve thee seven years for Rachel thy younger daughter." The record gives us a brief glimpse into Jacob's heart during these years; they seemed unto him but a few days, for the love he had to her. Oh, how he loved her!

The seven years passed, and Jacob came to claim his beautiful Rachel. An evening wedding was arranged; the bride came out heavily veiled. The wedding night passed, and in the cruel light of day Jacob saw his bride—Leah!

But Laban was right there to explain everything. "I forgot to tell you, Jacob, that in our country it is the custom that the oldest daughter must be married first. I forgot to tell you that. You will have to take her first."

May I say to you, this student was beginning to learn now. This was really his first big lesson. He refused submission to God at home, and he now submitted to his uncle in a far country. Jacob had deceived his father; he had stolen the blessing of the firstborn, now he had been deceived because of the right of the firstborn. He was learning the truth of the old saying, "Chickens come home to

ENVOYS QUARTET

From
MINNEAPOLIS, MINNESOTA

SPECIAL MUSIC**********
****THE GOSPEL IN WORD

Pastor Doyle Vaughn   291-5399

roost." They always do. And you will find that God puts it in different language later on: "Be not deceived; God is not mocked: for whatsoever a man soweth, that shall he also reap" (Gal 6:7).

Jacob deceived his old father about the favorite son, and many years later, when he himself was old, his sons brought to him the coat of Joseph, his favorite son, dipped in blood, the blood of goats, to deceive him into believing that his son had been slain. It is arresting to notice that every crooked thing this man did came back to him in the same coin. The Word of God promises that it will work that way.

After Jacob had been tricked into marrying Leah, he served seven more years to get Rachel. He served an additional six years to get his sheep. After dealing with Laban for twenty years, he took his leave; and Laban took out after him. Laban would have put him to death had not God intervened. When he caught up with Jacob, he stormed, "What do you mean by taking my daughters and taking my grandchildren? You didn't even let me kiss them good-bye."

But Jacob defended his action; listen to his wail: "Thus have I been twenty years in thy house; I served thee fourteen years for thy two daughters, and six years for thy cattle: and thou hast changed my wages ten times" (Gen 31:41).

Jacob was through at Haran now. He had had an excellent education and had finished all of Uncle Laban's courses.

Jacob resumed his journey, and one memorable night he was left alone to wrestle with God.

I was very interested, several years ago, in a letter in *Time* magazine which had come from a reader, a major down in Texas. He had written relative to something that had appeared in the magazine. His letter read, "In *Time* magazine you said that not a vote went to the most famous athlete in history, Wrestling Jacob. I've followed sports all my life but I never heard of Jacob. Can you tell me something about him?" Imagine, a major in the United States army knowing nothing about Jacob! May I say, however, that Jacob was not much of a wrestler. He honestly did not want to wrestle. Behind him was his aggrieved Uncle Laban, ahead of him was his brother, Esau, who, the last time he saw him, was threatening his life. If you think Jacob wanted to take on a third man that night, you are wrong.

Although Jacob did not want to wrestle, the angel wrestled with him. The angel, I believe, was none other than the preincarnate Christ. *God* wrestled with Jacob that night. God crippled him and let him know that he was His man and could not continue to live as he had been living. You see, God will let the prodigal son get into the pig pen, but God will never permit a prodigal son to continue to live in the pig pen. If he is a son, and not a pig, someday he will arise and go back to his father's house. Jacob was God's man, and God crippled him there that night. I wish I could say that he learned his lesson, but he did not.

The next day he met Esau, and discovered that he was not angry at all. Thus Esau revealed himself to be a bigger man than Jacob. Esau invited him to make his home with him, but Jacob did not want to live near his brother. He had somthing else in mind.

As soon as Esau had turned his back and started home, Jacob took his family down to Shechem. It was a tragic move—Jacob was still depending upon his own cleverness. His daughter, Dinah, was raped; and Simeon and Levi, her full brothers, went into the city of Shechem to the prince who was responsible. Though he wanted to marry her, they murdered him; and the sons of Jacob conducted a slaughter that would make a gang shooting in Chicago look pretty tame.

When they returned home, Jacob said, "You've made my name to smell among the people of my own land." He should not have gone to Shechem. But he learned his lesson.

Some believers still have to learn that sin will catch up with them. It always does. God said this in Galatians 6:7-8. "Whatsoever a man soweth, that shall he also reap. For he that soweth to his flesh shall of the flesh reap corruption; but he that soweth to the Spirit shall of the Spirit reap life everlasting." You sow corn, you reap corn; you sow wheat, you reap wheat; you sow cotton, you reap cotton; you sow sin, you reap sin. You reap exactly what you sow. Old Jacob, when he left Shechem a brokenhearted man, knew then that whatever a man sows he will reap.

"And God said unto Jacob, Arise, go up to Bethel, and dwell there: and make there an altar unto God, that appeared unto thee when thou fleddest from the face of Esau thy brother" (Gen 35:1). God called him back to Bethel, back to a fresh start, a new year.

"Then Jacob said unto his household, and to all that were with him, Put away the strange gods that are among you, and be clean, and change your garments" (Gen 35:2). Rachel, you recall, had taken the idols from her parental home and had concealed them while Laban searched the entire camp. I suppose she continued to worship those idols, for she had come from a home of idolatry. Jacob loved her and was too indulgent with her. It seems that idolatry was an accepted part of family life. Now God says, "Go back to Bethel. That's where I started with you, Jacob. You have to go back."

You have to be clean. That means confession of sins. My friend, you have to deal with sin in your life. Don't think that you can just rub out the sins of this past year. You are dealing with God. You've got to confess your sin. God has said, "If we confess our sins, he is faithful and just to forgive us our sins, and to cleanse us from all unrighteousness" (1 Jn 1:9). He will cleanse you today. You cannot go back to Bethel unless you clean up. That is what it means.

Then, change your garments. Garments in Scripture are habits. We use the same expression today when we speak of riding habits or walking habits. Jacob was God's man, he was going to change his garments, his habits, and start living differently. And, as far as I can tell, from the day he went back to Bethel, he started living for God.

Jacob said to his family, "And let us arise, and go up to Bethel; and I will make there an altar unto God, who answered me in the day of my distress, and was with me in the way which I went" (Gen 35:3). He remembered that, running away from home, homesick and lonesome, he had come to Bethel; and God had appeared to him. God had said, "I'll be faithful to you." But Jacob had gone on his way, not depending on God's faithfulness but on his own ability. He fell on his face; disappointment and tragedy came to him. Yet through it all, God was with him; and God blessed him. Now He says, "Go back to Bethel. You have to go back to where you started, Jacob. You have to go back."

How about you, my friend? Do you have a Bethel in your past? Do you remember the day you came to Christ? It was exciting, wasn't it! You were filled with wonder. Thrilling times those were! You may have wandered far since then. You may be at this moment actually away from God, living by your own wits, trusting in your own ability. Perhaps your life even blends in with the lives of those in the world.

Joseph Lewis Preston, of the Free Thinkers of America, told an Associated Press reporter, "Organized interest in atheism has lagged because the opposition isn't as strong as it used to be. There has been considerable liberalizing of religion and the lines of conflict aren't nearly as strong." Charles Smith, president of the American Association for the Advancement of Atheism, reported that the lack of opposition was the cause of the decline of atheism. "We don't have the old repressive religion that stimulates atheism, and they don't preach hell-fire and Jonah in the whale anymore. They go in for this cheer-them-up religion. That's not the old-time religion. It may be that this new sort is not so bad, but they don't let it interfere with their lives. They spent more time in the old days pleasing God. Now they try to please their fellow men."

Is not this an awful commentary on the Christian today? Yet in spite of it all, God has blessed. Remember how it was with you at the beginning. You did not have much then, materially speaking. But you had fellowship with your God. I call you back to Bethel today, back to the house of God.

Put away your idols.

You may protest, "You're wrong, preacher, we don't have any idols." Are you sure you don't? Materialism and secularism are our idols today. To some of you, your home is your idol—you have spent more in redecorating your home this past year than you have spent for God's work. And at the same time, you speak of looking for the Lord to come. Your neighbors know you don't mean it.

Some have made pleasure an idol. Actually your interest in the church is in the entertainment it offers. You do not go to pray; you do not go to study the Word of God: you go to be entertained.

Some have made a television your god. You spend more time in front of it on Sunday nights than you spend in the house of God. To some of you, business has become your idol, and you have no time for your God.

Some of you have made a child or your family or even church activity your idol. Good things, you know, can keep you from the best things.

Put away your strange gods if you are going back to Bethel.

Be clean. There will have to be confession of sin.

Change your garments; change your habits.

Come back to Bethel, the house of God, back to the ladder which is access to God, to fellowship with Him.

"So Jacob came to Luz, which is in the land of Canaan,

that is, Bethel, he and all the people that were with him.
And he built there an altar, and called the place Elbethel
[God of the house of God]: because there God appeared
unto him, when he fled from the face of his brother. . . .

"And God appeared unto Jacob again, when he came
out of Padanaram, and blessed him. And God said unto
him, Thy name is Jacob [Supplanter]: thy name shall
not be called any more Jacob, but Israel [Prince with
God] shall be thy name: and he called his name Israel. . . .

"And God went up from him in the place where he
talked with him. . . . And Jacob called the name of the
place where God spake with him, Bethel" (Gen 35:6-7,
9-10, 13, 15).

3

HIS DREAMS CAME TRUE

Joseph

Genesis 37, 39-45

The beginning of our story goes way back in the life of Joseph to the time he was a teenager and had two dreams: "And Joseph dreamed a dream, and he told it his brethren: and they hated him yet the more. . . . Behold, we were binding sheaves in the field, and, lo, my sheaf arose, and also stood upright; and, behold, your sheaves stood round about, and made obeisance to my sheaf. . . . Behold, I have dreamed a dream more; and, behold, the sun and the moon and the eleven stars made obeisance to me" (Gen 37:5, 7, 9).

These dreams so incurred the jealousy and hatred of his brothers that they sold him into slavery. This begins his "from rags to riches" story. No drama either ancient or modern is more thrilling than the life of Joseph. There is no person in the Old Testament in whose life the purposes of God are more clearly seen. The hand of God was upon him, and the leading of the Lord is evident, but Joseph is the one patriarch to whom God did not appear directly (according to the text of Scripture). God appeared to Abraham, Isaac, and Jacob, but not to Joseph. Yet the direction of God in his life is more evident than in any other. He is the Old Testament example of Romans 8:28, "And we know that all things work together for good to

them that love God, to them who are the called according
to his purpose." In fact, Joseph recognized this, and so
expressed it to his brothers in Genesis 50:20, "But as for
you, ye thought evil against me; but God meant it unto
good, to bring to pass, as it is this day, to save much people alive."

When he was young, everything seemed to go wrong in
his life, and everyone seemed to work against him. He had
several heartbreaking reverses and bitter disappointments,
but God brought Joseph through all these by His providential dealings to a most enviable position: "And Pharaoh
said unto Joseph, See, I have set thee over all the land of
Egypt. And Pharaoh took off his ring from his hand, and
put it upon Joseph's hand, and arrayed him in vestures of
fine linen, and put a gold chain about his neck; . . . and
they cried before him, Bow the knee: and he made him
ruler over all the land of Egypt. And Pharaoh said unto
Joseph, I am Pharaoh, and without thee shall no man lift
up his hand or foot in all the land of Egypt" (Gen 41:41-
44).

We pick up the narrative of the life of Joseph at the
point when his ten brothers, because of the press of the
famine, make a trip down to the land of Egypt to buy
grain. "And Joseph's ten brethren went down to buy grain
in Egypt. . . . And Joseph was the governor over the land,
and he it was that sold to all the people of the land: and
Joseph's brethren came, and bowed down themselves before him with their faces to the earth" (Gen 42:3, 6,
NSRB).

Joseph had been the one who had accumulated, during
the seven years of plenty, all of the surplus grain. He
filled, I suppose, all the granaries and built others in the
land of Egypt, because the entire world was fed from them
for seven years. People came from everywhere around the
Mediterranean, and especially Africa and Asia, into Egypt
to get grain.

One day as Joseph is going through the line giving certain permission (I suppose there were those who were not given permission), he looks and sees his ten brothers, those who had sold him into Egyptian slavery. He sees them bowing down before him. You can imagine the reaction of this man when he first recognizes them. I'm sure that the reaction of many of us would be to strike back at them, but you will find that Joseph does not do that at all. That was neither his thought nor intent. However, he does intend to give his brothers a test, and he is rather hard on them at first.

Actually twenty years have passed by. He was seventeen years old when they sold him into slavery; he was thirty years old when he was brought before Pharaoh, and seven years of plenty had passed, so now he is about thirtyseven years of age. It was sometime during this period of seven years of drought that the brothers came down, and evidently near the beginning of it, maybe not the first year, but the second or the third year.

Now Joseph sees them. They do not think, of course, that he is even alive. He is the last person that they expect to see in Egypt next to Pharaoh in authority. They hadn't seen him since he was a teenager. Now he is a mature man, dressed like an Egyptian and speaking like an Egyptian. They have no idea he is Joseph, but he recognizes them immediately.

Here begins one of the most dramatic sections of the Word of God. There is nothing to compare to it except what happened on the cross, and you and I do not see that, because God put the mantle of darkness down over it. But we can see this scene, and it is tremendous.

Joseph tests his brothers: "And Joseph remembered the dreams which he dreamed of them." He had said that they were going to bow down to him. His father had rebuked him and dismissed it as an impossibility. Now it is actually taking place. His dreams have come true. "And said unto them, Ye are spies; to see the nakedness of the land ye are come" (Gen 42:9). He makes an accusation against them that he knows is not true. He is drawing them out, as you can see. He is testing them. "And they said, Thy servants are twelve brethren, the sons of one man in the land of Canaan; and, behold, the youngest is this day with our father" (v. 13). Now Joseph is interested in the youngest because the youngest is his full brother. These men are half brothers, but the one who was not with them, Benjamin, is the son of his mother, Rachel. And you can see now why he is harsh with them. He is driving toward a very definite goal, and here it is: "Hereby ye shall be tested: by the life of Pharaoh ye shall not go forth from there, except your youngest brother come here" (v. 15, NSRB). What is it he wants? He wants to see his own brother, Benjamin. They say that he is back with the father, so he knows that he is alive, and he wants very much to see him. Observe him as he continues to move: "And he put them all together into prison three days. And Joseph said unto them the third day, This do, and live; for I fear God" (vv. 17-18, NSRB). That might have startled them coming from a pagan Egyptian. It would certainly startle you if you heard it from some governments today, by the way.

There is a strange and mysterious parallel between Joseph and Jesus that is nowhere mentioned in the Word of God. Although in the Bible there is not a scintilla of suggestion of this parallel, no one is more like Christ in his person and experience than Joseph.

JOSEPH	JESUS
Miraculous birth (Gen 30:22)	Virgin birth (Lk 1:35)
Loved by his father	Loved by His Father, "This is my beloved Son"
Set apart by coat of many colors	"Separate from sinners"
Announced he was to rule over his brethren	Presented Himself as the Messiah
Sent to his brethren	Sent to His brethren
Hated by his brethren without a cause	Hated by His brethren without a cause

Obeyed his father	Obeyed His Father
Sent by his father to seek his brethren	Sent by His Father to seek His brethren
Mocked by his brethren, "Behold this dreamer cometh."	Mocked by His brethren
Sold by his brethren	Sold by one of His brethren
Sold for twenty pieces of silver	Sold for thirty pieces of silver
Plotted against by his brethren	Plotted against by His brethren to kill Him
Put in pit (death)	Crucified
Raised up	Raised up the third day
Not received	Not received
His bloody coat returned to his father	His coat taken and gambled for
After being sold into Egypt, lost sight of for many years	Ascended up into heaven, "And ye shall see me no more"
Tempted by the world, the flesh, and the devil; and resisted them	Tempted by the world, the flesh, and the devil; and won
Became the savior of the world during this period (from physical death)	Is the Saviour of the world today (from spiritual death)
While on Pharaoh's throne, gave bread to the world	Is the bread of life
His brethren had to leave the promised land	Jews scattered today
Not recognized at first by brethren	Not recognized today by brethren.
Took a Gentile bride while rejected	Is calling out the Church, His bride, during His rejection
Made himself known unto his brethren	Will make Himself known unto His brethren
His repentant brethren reconciled to him	Christ's brethren are to repent and be reconciled to Him (Zec 13:6; 12:10)
Forgave and received his brethren	Will forgive and receive His brethren
Shared his glory with his brethren	His brethren will share His glory

I'd like to pick up the parallel at this particular point. You will notice that Joseph put them in prison for three days; then on the third day he brought them out and gave them life, saying, "This do, and live: for I fear God." The third day suggests to any Christian the day the Lord Jesus came back from the dead, and it is through His death and resurrection that life and liberty are offered to men today. Listen to Him in John 11:25-26. Before He raised Lazarus from the dead and before He Himself was raised from the dead, He said this to the two sisters in Bethany: "I am the resurrection, and the life: he that believeth in me, though he were dead, yet shall he live. And whosoever liveth and believeth in me shall never die. Believeth thou this?"

There is offered life today to this world through the death and resurrection of Christ. And this is what Joseph offers to his brethren. When he first puts them in prison, I can tell you their thoughts were dark thoughts. Spies in that day would go from prison to their death. That would have to be their sentence. And they expected to be put to death. Then all of a sudden on the third day they are brought out, and this man says, "I fear God; therefore I offer you life."

At Christ's first coming, He offered life, and at the first coming of the brethren of Joseph they are offered life when they could have easily been put to death. Now these men feel there is a sentence over them, and each one has a guilty conscience. Listen to them: "And they said one to another, We are verily guilty concerning our brother, in that we saw the anguish of his soul, when he besought us, and we would not hear; therefore is this distress come upon us" (Gen 42:21). They are recalling the time when they were young men tending their father's flocks, and their kid brother, Joseph, came to them wearing his coat of many colors, which set him apart as their father's favorite. Their hatred flared, and they took him and put him in a pit. The narrative tells us that they sat down and ate as they discussed how to dispose of him, though they heard the anguish of his soul. You can hear this seventeen-year-old boy pleading for his life, but they hate him so much that they are determined to get rid of him. Now this has troubled them all these years. Here in a foreign land, when their lives seem to be in jeopardy, they acknowledge their crime, and Joseph hears their confession.

It reminds us of a statement of Moses in Numbers 32:23: "Be sure your sin will find you out." Ordinarily this is interpreted to mean that your sin is going to be found out, that somebody will find out about it. Well, there is an element of truth in that, of course, but that is not what this verse says. Rather it says that your sin will find *you* out. Though you may commit a sin, and we're living in a day where there is an attempt to throw off all restraint, your conscience will torment you at night. There are many folk today who are entertaining a very bad conscience because of sin in their lives. These brothers of Joseph had that experience.

"And they knew not that Joseph understood them; for he spoke unto them by an interpreter" (v. 23). You see, to each other they speak in Hebrew, never suspecting that this Egyptian understands their language. But Joseph uses an interpreter so they will not suspect that he understands them.

May I say to you that you and I are dealing today with a Saviour who understands us. I do not know why a great many people think that their lives are hidden from God. The psalmist speaks of secret sins being open in His presence: "Shall not God search this out? For he knoweth the secrets of the heart" (Ps 44:21). As someone has said, "Secret sin down here is open scandal in heaven." And John makes this statement concerning Jesus: "And needed not that any should testify of man: for he knew what was in man" (Jn 2:25). You remember that on many occasions without the enemy saying a word, He interpreted their thoughts and answered the thing that was in their thinking. And, my friend, this day He knows you and He knows me as no one else knows us.

What a picture we have here as these brothers speak in a language that they think Joseph does not understand. Notice Joseph's reaction: "And he turned himself about

from them, and wept" (v. 24). You can see the pent-up
emotion in this man. He can no longer restrain himself.
He wants to make himself known to them, but he must test
them, and so he excuses himself for a moment while he
goes aside and weeps. Then he returns to them and continues in this very harsh manner: "And took from them
Simeon, and bound him before their eyes." He keeps
Simeon there as a hostage while he permits the other
brothers to return home. These men have confessed their
crime, but he is going to test them further.

Joseph keeps Simeon as a hostage; the others are free
to go. This is substitution—as Jesus bore the sins of many
that you and I might go free.

"Then Joseph commanded to fill their sacks with grain,
and to restore every man's money into his sack, and to
give them provision for the way; and thus did he unto
them" (v. 25, NSRB). When they reached the inn, the
first man to open his sack found that his money had been
refunded and was there in the sack. And, my beloved,
continuing to follow through with the parallel, salvation,
life, and liberty today are available without money and
without price. Salvation is free! It is not cheap; it cost
God a great deal, but to us it is free.

"And it came to pass as they emptied their sacks, that,
behold, every man's bundle of money was in his sack:
and when both they and their father saw the bundles of
money, they were afraid" (v. 35). They didn't understand,
of course, and they were afraid. Also the average church
member today just cannot see how God can save by His
grace. He wants to do something to gain God's favor. My
friend, you can do nothing today to merit His favor. What
Jesus did for you on the cross was to make it possible for
a holy God to reach down and to save you. You cannot
add to that. The refunded money is a marvelous, wonderful
picture of this fact.

These boys return to their father and recount their experience in Egypt. The reaction of old Jacob is quite in-

teresting: "And Jacob, their father, said unto them, Me have ye bereaved of my children: Joseph is not, and Simeon is not, and ye will take Benjamin away: all these things are against me" (v. 36).

Over this I see the shadow of Rachel because when this youngest boy was born, Rachel was dying, and she looked at the little fellow and called his name Ben-oni, meaning "the son of my sorrow." But when Jacob saw his dead Rachel and saw this little fellow who looked like her, he said, "No, we'll call him Benjamin; he's the son of my right hand." He leaned upon this boy. He was his walking stick the rest of the way through life. Jacob says, "You mean to tell me that man down in Egypt wants my youngest son to come down? That can never take place." Well, it had to take place because the famine, we read in chapter 43, "was severe in the land."

"And it came to pass, when they had eaten up the grain which they had brought out of Egypt, their father said unto them, Go again, buy us a little food" (v. 2, NSRB). Judah comes forward and he says, "Listen, Dad, that man meant business. He told us not to come down unless we brought our youngest brother. He is keeping Simeon down there, and he'll take his life if we don't bring Benjamin down." Jacob sees that he has to release the boy. So he entrusts him to their care.

Here now is the most dramatic scene of this dramatic narrative.

"And the men took that present, and they took double money in their hand, and Benjamin; and rose up, and went down to Egypt, and stood before Joseph" (v. 15). And when Joseph saw Benjamin with them, he said to the ruler of his house, Bring these men home, and slaughter an animal, and make ready; for these men shall dine with me at noon" (v. 16, NSRB).

This is a frightening development. They wonder what is up. "Why in the world did he invite us home for dinner?" The steward of Joseph's house reassures them:

"And he said, Peace be to you, fear not: your God, and the God of your father, hath given you treasure in your sacks: I had your money. And he brought Simeon out unto them" (v. 23). All of this is to comfort them. He releases Simeon, and says, "Forget about the money. It's all right."

Later Joseph comes home and begins to ask questions. Listen to him: "And he asked them of their welfare, and said, Is your father well, the old man of whom ye spoke? Is he yet alive? And they answered, Thy servant, our father, is in good health, he is yet alive. And they bowed down their heads, and made obeisance" (vv. 27-28). Here they go down on all fours before Joseph.

"And he lifted up his eyes, and saw his brother Benjamin, his mother's son, and said, Is this your younger brother, of whom ye spoke unto me?" (v. 29). Here is this young man—I think that he looked like his mother Rachel, and Joseph recognized him immediately although he didn't want them to know yet. "And he said, God be gracious unto thee, my son. And Joseph made haste; for his heart yearned over his brother" (vv. 29-30, NSRB). He wanted to go and throw his arms around his brother.

"And he sought where to weep; and he entered into his chamber, and wept there. And he washed his face, and went out, and controlled himself; and said, Set on bread" (vv. 30-31, NSRB). Dinner is ready. And as the fellows go to the table, they are startled to see that they are seated according to age, from Reuben, the oldest, right down to Benjamin. The brothers look at one another in amazement. "How did he know?" "How could he know?"

Now notice his feeling for his young brother: "And he took and sent messes unto them from before him: but Benjamin's mess was five times so much as any of theirs. And they drank, and were merry with him" (v. 34). They now are having a wonderful time together.

Joseph does not yet reveal himself to his brothers. He takes his cup and places it in the sack of Benjamin. He now is going to test his brothers in respect to Benjamin. You see, they had been willing to sell *him* into slavery. What will they do for Benjamin? So after they have departed, he sends his steward out after them, saying that his master's cup had been stolen, and they were suspects. Judah is so sure they do not have it that he says, "With whomsoever of thy servants it be found, both let him die, and we also will be my lord's bondmen" (44:9).

A search was made and they found it in Benjamin's sack! What will his brothers do? With evident grief, they reload their animals and all return to face Joseph. Judah is the spokesman for the group, and I break into his plea at this point: "And it came to pass when we came up unto thy servant my father, we told him the words of my lord. And our father said, Go again, and buy us a little food. And we said, We cannot go down: if our youngest brother be with us, then will we go down; for we may not see the man's face, except our youngest brother be with us. And thy servant my father said unto us, Ye know that my wife bare me two sons: and the one went out from me, and I said, Surely he is torn in pieces; and I saw him not since. And if ye take this also from me, and mischief befall him, ye shall bring down my gray hairs with sorrow to the grave" (vv. 24-29). He concludes by saying that he will take Benjamin's place: "For thy servant became surety for the lad unto my father, saying, If I bring him not unto thee, then I shall bear the blame to my father for ever. Now therefore, I pray thee, let thy servant abide instead of the lad a bondman to my lord; and let the lad go up with his brethren" (vv. 32-33).

That is too much for Joseph. He has tested them now, and they have stood the test. "Then Joseph could not refrain himself before all them who stood by him; and he cried, Cause every man to go out from me. And there stood no man with him, while Joseph made himself known unto his brethren. And he wept aloud; and the Egyptians and the house of Pharaoh heard. And Joseph said unto his brethren, I am Joseph; doth my father yet live? And his brethren could not answer him; for they were troubled at his presence. And Joseph said unto his brethren, Come near to me, I pray you. And they came near. And he said, I am Joseph, your brother, whom ye sold into Egypt" (45:1-4).

It was at the second coming that Joseph made himself known to his brethren. Stephen, as he recites their history in Acts 7:13, is very careful to make this distinction: "And at the second time Joseph was made known to his brethren; and Joseph's kindred was made known unto Pharaoh." At the second coming of these brethren, they knew who he was.

Notice the parallel. Our Lord came the first time. They rejected Him and crucified Him. But at the second coming of Christ (after the rapture and the Tribulation), He will return to this earth, and He will make Himself known unto His brethren. See this in Zechariah 12:10-12: "And I will pour upon the house of David, and upon the inhabitants of Jerusalem, the spirit of grace and of supplications: and they shall look upon me whom they have pierced, and they shall mourn for him, as one mourneth for his only son, and shall be in bitterness for him, as one that is in bitterness for his firstborn. In that day shall there be a great mourning in Jerusalem. . . . And the land shall mourn, every family apart."

This describes the great mourning that is coming when Christ returns the second time and reveals Himself unto Israel. Again in chapter 13, Zechariah speaks of this event: "And one shall say unto him, What are these wounds in thine hands? Then he shall answer, Those with which I was wounded in the house of my friends" (v. 6).

You see, they will ask about the nail prints in His hands, for He will still have them. And He will explain, "When I was here before, you crucified Me." That is when they will weep and mourn. We are told: "In that day there shall be a fountain opened to the house of David and to the inhabitants of Jerusalem for sin and for uncleanness" (v. 1).

What a picture is given to us here of that which is still future. Christ came the first time in weakness, in meekness, in obscurity. He will come the next time in power to assert His will over all the earth; and before Him every knee shall bow.

At His first coming He dealt with one question and one alone—the sin question, to die for the sins of the world. As Joseph saved the world from physical death, Christ came to deliver us from spiritual death. When He comes the second time, He will solve the governmental problems, the political and social dilemmas that harass our world. But up to this moment He deals only with the issue of sin in your heart and in mine.

"For ye know the grace of our Lord Jesus Christ, that, though he was rich, yet for your sakes he became poor, that ye through his poverty might be rich" (2 Co 8:9).

4

BATTLE OF THE GODS

Moses

Exodus 9-12

It was the Sunday after V-J Day (the day, you will recall, that was supposed to have ended World War II). I was then a pastor, and I chose for my subject, "The War Is Not Over." The message was truer than I possibly could have dreamed it would be.

However I was not speaking of a conflict between two armies wearing two different uniforms. I was not speaking at all of a physical conflict but of a spiritual conflict, a conflict about which Paul writes: "We wrestle not against flesh and blood, but against principalities, against powers, against the rulers of the darkness of this world, against spiritual wickedness in high places" (Eph 6:12). And he expressed it thus in his second letter to the Corinthians: "For though we walk in the flesh, we do not war after the flesh" (2 Co 10:3).

A spiritual struggle is going on today, a struggle that is behind every physical struggle. It is that which was actually responsible for World War II. It was responsible for the Korean conflict. It was responsible for the conflict in Vietnam. And it has been the cause of every war from the day that Abraham went down to deliver his nephew Lot from the cities of the plain. It is responsible for that which is labelled race riots in America, which are not a conflict between black and white, or between civil rights and civil wrongs.

There is a spiritual conflict behind every physical conflict today. And this spiritual conflict is between light and darkness, between good and evil, between heaven and hell. It ultimately is between God and Satan. It began before man was ever created; it will continue here on this earth even after the Church is removed. It is more far-reaching than man can comprehend; it is deeper and wider than this earth. It's supercolossal; it is hypercosmic; it's extramundane. It is titanic, gigantic, and volcanic, if you please.

In the Scriptures, every now and then, it surfaces. It comes into sharp focus in the Word of God, and you can see it plainly. You can see it in the Garden of Eden, when the conflict was first joined there as far as man is concerned. Then you see it in the lives of two men who were twins, Jacob and Esau. You see it again taking place in the soul of that man Job as he fought his battle. You see it when God said, "The Lord will have warfare with Amalek from generation to generation" (Ex 17:16). There would be no peace; there would have to be a surrender. You see it in the conflict between Saul and David and between David and Goliath. You see it joined on the top of Mount Carmel when Elijah met the prophets of Baal. You see it in the temptation of the Lord Jesus in the wilderness. It is that of which Paul wrote, "The flesh lusteth against the Spirit, and the Spirit against the flesh; and these are contrary the one to the other" (Gal 5:17). Paul again mentions it in telling of the great things that were happening in Ephesus: "For a great door and effectual is opened unto me, and there are many adversaries" (1 Co 16:9).

One of the outstanding examples of this conflict was between Moses and Pharaoh. It had to do with the deliverance of Israel from Egyptian bondage.

The deliverance of Israel from the land and the hand of

Pharaoh is one of the great episodes recorded in the Word of God. The family of Jacob, numbering seventy, went down into the land of Egypt. They were welcome in Egypt because there was a friendly Pharaoh on the throne, one of the Hyksos kings (Bedouins who had come from the desert, of the same background as old Jacob).

Afterward that dynasty was overthrown, and the Egyptians came back into power. The Egyptians saw the people of Israel (who had become a multitude in the land of Egypt, probably 1½ million) as potential enemies, and reduced them to slavery.

For four hundred thirty years they were down there in the land of Egypt. God was silent. Seemingly He had put them down there, then went off and left them. But at the appointed time God returned to them. He remembered His promise to Abraham, Isaac, and Jacob.

"And the Lord said, I have surely seen the affliction of my people which are in Egypt, and have heard their cry by reason of their taskmasters; for I know their sorrows; and I am come down to deliver them out of the hand of the Egyptians" (Ex 3:7-8a). God came back to deliver them. After forty years' absence from Egypt, Moses appeared back in the land. God had trained him to be the leader. God was ready. Moses was to assemble the elders of Israel, and all together they were to go to Pharaoh. Pharaoh's refusal would open the struggle. And the struggle, my beloved, was not to be just between two men, Pharaoh and Moses. Pharaoh was the representative of the gods of Egypt, and the battle was joined there. Notice the language of Exodus 12:12: "Against all the gods of Egypt I will execute judgment: I am the LORD." In these plagues that God brought onto Egypt, He was executing judgment against the gods of Egypt, against the idolatry of the land.

That leads me to say that there is actually a fourfold reason why God brought the judgments upon the land of Egypt. The first, as I've already indicated, is that Egypt was dominated by idolatry. Egypt had thousands of temples and millions of idols. Memphis was the ancient capital of Egypt. It, at one time, shared honors with Thebes up in the upper Nile, but Memphis is the long-time capital. It was a mass of huge temples. It was a city eight miles long, four miles wide, a large city for that day, one of the largest of the ancient cities. It had a tremendous population and had more temples and idols than any place has ever had on topside of this earth.

If you think that there was no power in idolatry, I do not think that you have examined the evidence. There was power in this false religion. It is the thing to which Paul calls our attention in his letter to Timothy: "Now as Jannes and Jambres withstood Moses, so do these also resist the truth: men of corrupt minds, reprobate concerning the faith" (2 Ti 3:8).

The magicians of Egypt were able to duplicate the miracles that Moses and Aaron performed; that is, the first three. When Moses threw down his rod in the presence of Pharaoh and it became a serpent, the magicians of Egypt did it also. When Moses turned the Nile into blood, they duplicated it. And when he brought the frogs up, they duplicated that. But after that they fled, saying, "This is the finger of God" (Ex 8:19). However, in their heathen religion there was power, satanic power. Satan, I believe, gave power to all the pagan, heathen religions of the past.

This is what I mean. The Greeks were a highly civilized people. You cannot read anything that comes out of that one hundred years of the Periclean Age, with its culture and its achievements, without realizing that those men were men of great ability. Yet those men worshiped gods, and they made trips to the Oracle of Delphi, and they got information. Do you think they got accurate information? I do not believe they would have been fooled by a fake. I believe that many times they got accurate information. How did they get it? May I say to you that Satan has been back of idolatry, as he is back of false cults today.

When someone says to me, "Oh, false cults are meaning-
less. They have nothing in them," he just thinks they
don't. They have tremendous power in them, but it is
satanic power, my beloved. And we need to recognize today that there are two great spiritual forces in this world—
that of God and that of Satan also. Satan's power is tremendous in this world. So the plagues were leveled at the
gods of Egypt. They were a telling blow against the idolatry of the Egyptian people.

There was a second reason that God brought the plagues
on Egypt. Listen to this language: "And the Egyptians
shall know that I am the LORD, when I stretch forth mine
hand upon Egypt, and bring out the children of Israel from
among them" (Ex 7:5). Another reason, therefore, for the
plagues was to convince the Egyptian people. Why was it
necessary to send ten plagues, and why did He drag them
out? Because, my beloved, even in the time of judgment
God was prepared to extend mercy. Every time Pharaoh
would seem to repent, immediately God called off the
plague. Why? Because God was prepared to extend mercy.
He gave them ten plagues, yes, but don't miss the fact that
those ten plagues were ten opportunities for the people of
Egypt to turn to God. And when we get to the book of
Numbers, we find that many of them did turn to God.
Also it is interesting to note that when the Gospel first
started out in the early Christian era, the center of Gospel
preaching was not Asia nor Europe: it was North Africa.
Four of the greatest men the Church has produced came
out of North Africa: Augustine, Tertullian, Origen, and
Athanasius. These men were in a land that had a long
history of God's judgment upon idolatry. God says, "I'll
convince the Egyptians." And, believe me, He did it.

Then there is a third reason for the plagues. We are told
that God had hardened Pharaoh's heart. For some reason,
that has caused more controversy than anything else in
this particular narrative. I have heard more people weep
over "poor Pharaoh," and have tried to exonerate him be-

cause God hardened his heart. It has certainly been misunderstood. What does it mean? The word in Hebrew means to twist with a rope. God twisted his heart; that's exactly what the Hebrew means. In effect God said, "This man Pharaoh, I know his heart, and I'll twist it and make come out of it what is there." He forced Pharaoh to make a decision. Have you noticed how vacillating Pharaoh was? One time he'd agree; the next time he would change his mind. A great many people are like that. They say, "Yes, I'll stand for God," but they don't. God brought Pharaoh right out and made him stand the test.

Let me illustrate. The sun shining down on this earth today will melt wax and it will harden clay. Are you going to say that the business of the sun is to melt? Then why does it harden clay? If you say the business of the sun is to harden, then why does it melt wax? Does the sun have a special built-in hardener and a built-in softener? No. The difference is due to the element that is put under its heat. All God is doing to Pharaoh is bringing *out* of his heart that which was *in* his heart. The Lord Jesus said, "Out of the heart proceed the issues of life." Then He names some of the things that come out of the heart, and I can't find a nice thing in the lot. The Old Testament had already said that. Jeremiah wrote (17:9), "The heart is deceitful above all things, and desperately wicked: who can know it?" And God was bringing out that which was in Pharaoh's heart. That is a purpose of the judgments.

Now there is a fourth and final reason for the plagues. It was to demonstrate to Israel that God could deliver. "And that thou mayest tell in the ears of thy son, and of thy son's son, what things I have wrought in Egypt, and my signs which I have done among them; that ye may know how that I am the LORD" (Ex 10:2). God must demonstrate to His own people that He could deliver them. Remember that they had been born in the brickyards of Egypt. They were idolaters. In the wilderness when Moses was away from them, they immediately made a golden

calf and worshiped it. (You know, it took God only one
night to get them out of Egypt, but it took Him forty years
to get Egypt out of them. Likewise with us, God saves us
instantly, but it takes Him a long time to get the world out
of us, and some of us are still in the process.)

God moved in and so demonstrated His power in delivering the Israelites that the memory of it would be
passed down from generation to generation. God says,
"You'll be able to tell your sons, and then when your
grandson comes along you can put him on your knee and
say, 'Look, this is what God did for us when we were slaves
down in the land of Egypt. I had worked all day in the
brickyards, and when I got home, weary and tired because
I didn't have straw for the bricks, Moses said to be ready,
that we were going out that very night. Do you think we
could escape that tremendous army of Pharaoh? Of course
we couldn't! But we had already seen evidences of God's
hand, and that night God led us out. And we went across
the Red Sea on dry land, and on into that wilderness. We
still were a stiffnecked people, but our God was faithful to
us.' " God was demonstrating to His people, who had fallen
into the idolatry of Egypt, that He was their God.

It was a definite, deliberate, designed attack upon idolatry which would have a message for Pharaoh; it would
have a message for the Egyptians; it would have a message
for the Israelites; and it would have a message for you
and me.

Now let's run through these plagues one by one, and see
their purpose and order. This came to my attention years
ago as a student in college and did more to lift my faith at
that time than anything else. I had always felt that the
plagues were haphazard, that whatever came to the mind
of the Lord He threw in. It wasn't that at all.

1. Blood

The first plague: the Nile River was turned to blood.
"And Moses and Aaron did so, as the Lord commanded;

and he lifted up the rod, and smote the waters that were in the river, in the sight of Pharaoh, and in the sight of his servants; and all the waters that were in the river were turned to blood" (Ex 7:20).

As Dr. Adams said, "Egypt is the Nile," and without the Nile, that country would be right back in the Libyan desert, not even fit for human habitation. Because of the Nile, Egypt has been the breadbasket of the world. God made it that way. But instead of the blessing God had intended, the Nile became that which these people worshiped.

It is interesting to note that there were four sources of religion in the land of Egypt, and all four can be traced back to monotheism, that there is one living and true God. But there came a day when, though "they knew God, they glorified him not as God, neither were thankful, but became vain in their imaginations, and their foolish heart was darkened" (Ro 1:21). They began to serve the thing created rather than the Creator. They began to worship the Nile River.

The Nile was sacred to Osiris. I'm sure you have seen in a great deal of the paintings of Egypt, especially found in the tombs, that all-seeing eye with rays radiating from it. That is the eye of Osiris, and the Nile River was sacred to Osiris.

The fertility of the land depended upon the Nile River and its overflowing every year. But when the Nile was turned to blood, that which was fertility became sterility. That which was life became death. At the very beginning, God struck at that which was the very lifeblood of Egypt and turned it to blood.

Although this first plague had its effect, it didn't change Pharaoh.

2. FROGS

The second plague was frogs. "And the LORD spoke unto Moses, Go unto Pharaoh, and say unto him, Thus

saith the LORD, Let my people go, that they may serve me.
And if thou refuse to let them go, behold, I will smite all
thy borders with frogs: and the river shall bring forth frogs
abundantly, which shall go up and come into thine house,
and into thy bedchamber, and upon thy bed, and into the
house of thy servants, and upon thy people, and into thine
ovens, and into thy kneading troughs" (Ex 8:1-3).

One of the most beautiful temples that was in Memphis
was the temple to Heka, the frog-headed goddess. Have
you ever seen a beautiful idol? When men apart from
revelation conceive of God they never think of Him as
being beautiful or wonderful or glorious, but absolutely
hideous. That is the way they have made images of Him.
All idols are that way. And in Egypt they worshiped the
ugly frog-headed goddess Heka. Frogs, naturally, were
sacred to Heka, and it was an offense in Egypt ever to kill
a frog. All along the Nile there were frogs, but nobody
killed them. They were sacred to Heka.

Imagine, my friend, having frogs in your living room,
frogs in your bedroom (and in your *bed*), frogs in the
kitchen and in your food—and not be able to kill them!
God has a sense of humor. God must have smiled at this
particular case. Frogs everywhere, and no one dared harm
one. They got all they wanted of the frog-headed goddess
Heka. No wonder Pharaoh called Moses to get rid of
them: *he* could not touch them; they could not.

3. LICE

The third plague was lice.

"And the LORD said unto Moses, Say unto Aaron,
Stretch out thy rod, and smite the dust of the land, that it
may become lice throughout all the land of Egypt" (Ex
8:16).

The Egyptians worshiped the earth-god, Geb. And lice,
it was thought, were made out of the dust of the earth.
Now the lice covered the land. This which was sacred to
Geb was something they could not touch. And the very

thing that they worshiped they now despised. They must walk upon them, they must destroy them, and they asked Moses to remove them from the land of Egypt.

4. FLIES

The fourth plague brought swarms of flies, more accurately, beetles, or, as we have thought of them in connection with the Egyptians, the scarab. "And the LORD did so; and there came a grievous swarm of flies into the house of Pharaoh, and into his servants' houses, and into all the land of Egypt: the land was corrupted by reason of the swarm of flies" (Ex 8:24).

You have seen, I am sure, pictures of the gold scarabs that have been found in the tombs of Egypt. Old King Tut was a third-rate king, but even he had gold scarabs in his tomb. They were sacred to Ra, the sun god. The disc that symbolized him has been found in the tombs and in many places in that land. He was one of the main gods that they worshiped. And Khepara was the beetle-god. They believed that in that beetle there was eternal life, which is the reason they put gold scarabs in the tombs. It was evidence that they were going to live forever.

Well, beetles in your tomb wouldn't bother you, but imagine them in bed with you! There is a certain amount of humor in these judgments.

5. MURRAIN

The next plague affected the cattle of Egypt. "And the LORD did that thing on the morrow, and all the cattle of Egypt died: but the cattle of the children of Israel died not one" (Ex 9:6). Egypt has been called the land of zoology. With a tour group I made a trip out to the pyramids. When we got back one of the men who knew the area said, "Did you see the mummies of the bulls?"

We said, "No."

"Well," he said, "you missed the most important thing." So several that were in our group went back out there to get pictures of them. Well, I was not interested in going twelve miles in all that heat to see mummies of bulls! But they are there—literally hundreds of them, reverently entombed in sarcophagi. Archaeologists have just begun to unearth them. What does it mean? It means simply that Apis, the black bull, was worshiped in Egypt. The second largest temple that Egypt ever built was located in Memphis and was for the worship of the black bull Apis.

God was hitting them in a vulnerable spot. Imagine worshiping a sick cow! God was striking them at the very center of their degrading idolatry.

6. Boils

God now closes in on them personally. "And the LORD said unto Moses and unto Aaron, Take to you handfuls of ashes of the furnace, and let Moses sprinkle it toward the heaven in the sight of Pharaoh. And it shall become small dust in all the land of Egypt, and shall be a boil breaking forth with blains upon man, and upon beast, throughout all the land of Egypt" (Ex 9:8-9). The priests of all the religions of Egypt had to be spotless in order to serve in the temples. They couldn't have any mark or blemish in their bodies whatsoever. Well, may I say to you, they had a moratorium on worship in Egypt during this period because of the boils that were on all the priests. None of them could serve anywhere. It was actually a judgment on the entire religion of the land of Egypt.

7. Hail

God begins now to demonstrate His power as He moves in with this judgment, "That thou mayest know that there is none like me in all the earth" (v. 14). "Behold, to morrow about this time I will cause it to rain a very grievous hail, such as hath not been in Egypt since the foundation thereof even until now" (Ex 9:18). Egypt was a land of no rain. In Cairo I asked a man there how much rainfall they had. He said, "We had an inch last year."

I said, "Is that normal?"

He said, "Yes."

"Well," I said, "that's not much rain."

He said, "You ought to go up the Nile; rain up there is a phenomenon. They just don't have it at all."

So here God is moving into an area where no one could move or would dare to move: He will control the rainfall. Rain comes in the form of hail, but it is a hail of judgment upon them. Their sky-goddess is powerless in her own domain.

8. Locusts

Then there was the judgment of the locusts, and that was against the insect gods. The way Egyptians worshiped insects and birds is the most amazing thing. No people have been more given over to it. We sometimes think that only in the dark heart of Africa could this worship exist, but it is nothing compared to that in the land of Egypt. In fact, evidently it filtered down from the north of Africa to all the tribes of Africa, and that is where they got the idea of worshiping even insects, which is an awful thing.

Insects, especially the locust, have been a judgment. God has used them. You find also in the prophecy of Joel and in the book of Revelation plagues of locusts which are yet to come.

"And the LORD said unto Moses, Stretch out thine hand over the land of Egypt for the locusts, that they may come up upon the land of Egypt, and eat every herb of the land, even all that the hail hath left" (Ex 10:12). God is making it clear that the judgment of the locusts is from Him.

9. Darkness

And then we come to the ninth judgment, which is judgment upon the sun-god Ra. Darkness comes over the land of Egypt in the daytime. God moves in with darkness against the chief god that they worshiped. The sun disc is the most familiar symbol the Egyptians used; it is in all of their art. It is to the sun-god Ra. The plague of darkness shows the utter helplessness of Ra. "And Moses stretched forth his hand toward heaven; and there was a thick darkness in all the land of Egypt three days: they saw not one another, neither rose any from his place for three days: but all the children of Israel had light in their dwellings" (Ex 10:22-23).

At this time also Pharaoh is abandoned. He has had opportunity to repent; he has not. Apparently many of the Egyptian people repent and turn to God, and they are spared. But Pharaoh will not repent. From here on Moses will appear to him no more. "He, that being often reproved hardeneth his neck, shall suddenly be destroyed, and that without remedy" (Pr 29:1).

10. DEATH OF THE FIRSTBORN

The tenth judgment is the last. God announces to His people and to the Egyptians that this will be the last. "After this," He says, "I'll take my people out." It is the death of the firstborn, not only the firstborn of man but of every creature. You will recall that God had said to His people that the firstborn belonged to Him. And that goes back to the Garden of Eden. In fact, that is the reason Eve named Cain; she said, "I've gotten *the* man, the deliverer. He's God's man." And from that day on the firstborn always belonged to God, was given to the service of God. The firstborn in all pagan, heathen lands were set aside for the service of the gods. In the land of Egypt, God was reaching in and claiming that which was His own.

May I say to you, friend, there are many parents living today in our affluent society who hesitate to give their children to God. Many Christians do not want their children to go as missionaries. They do not want them to make a sacrifice that is a real sacrifice.

It is a dangerous thing for a Christian to withhold his firstborn from God. God reaches in many times and takes that which is His own. He did mine, because I had not given her to Him. I know He does it that way.

That's what He did in the land of Egypt. He reached in and took that which was His own. That was His final word to the land of Egypt.

It was the battle of the gods. God demonstrated that He is the living and true God. The victory is His. Let me call your attention to one last verse: "And in very deed for this cause have I raised thee up, for to show in thee my power; and that my name may be declared throughout all the earth" (Ex 9:16). The world heard it in that day, my friend. God won the victory then.

However, that battle has been going on from that day to this, and it is going on at this moment. And whether you like it or not, you are in it. You are either on Christ's side or you are on Satan's side. Jesus said, "If you're not for Me, you are against Me." You must take sides.

Our victory is not one that we have won. I get a little tired of people talking of living the victorious life. We are not living it. The only victorious life that you and I are offered today is *His* life. He is the One who got the victory over the cross. He is the One who got the victory over death and over the grave. He's the One today who can give to you and to me a victory. And we can only say, "We are more than conquerors through him that loved us."

5

A PROPHET FOR PROFIT

Balaam

Numbers 22-25

Across the pages of Scripture there march men and women from all walks of life. The Holy Spirit customarily gives a cameo-sharp picture of each one of them. There is, generally, a clear delineation of character, which the Holy Spirit gives to us in few words.

But there are some exceptions to this. There are those who walk across the pages of Scripture who are not clear at all. Their character is fuzzy and hazy. Darkness hides their true nature. And we're apt to get, even from Scripture, a distorted and twisted understanding of them. We're not always sure that we have a correct estimation or evaluation of their character. Let me mention some of them. In the Old Testament, Cain, Esau, Balaam, Samson, Saul, and Absalom march across the pages of Scripture. We can't be sure about these men. And in the New Testament, there's the rich young ruler (we wonder if he ever came back to Christ), and there are Judas, Demas, Ananias, and Sapphira. These are characters who walk in the shadows.

One of these, Balaam, is one of those enigmatic and mysterious characters in the Word of God. Eleanor Herr Boyd has said of him, "He's one of the strangest characters of all in Scripture." The question arises, is Balaam a genuine prophet of God? Or is he a religious racketeer? It's difficult to answer. Is Balaam sincerely seeking to serve God? Or is he a fake; is he as phony as a three-dollar bill?

You be the judge. I'll attempt to tell you all that I can gather concerning him, and I've read everything that I could put my hands on, and I will let you decide concerning this man. I'm confident that a great many people, when they read Numbers 22, 23, 24, and 25, are ready to dismiss him as an unsavory and an unworthy character, not worth further consideration. But you can't do that. Even before you finish the Old Testament, Micah tells us that we're to remember him. Notice what the prophet says, "O my people, remember now what Balak king of Moab consulted, and what Balaam the son of Beor answered him from Shittim unto Gilgal, that ye may know the righteousness of the Lord" (Mic 6:5).

In other words, Micah says you can't forget him; you can't ignore him because he is a tremendous lesson for God's people. And the very interesting thing is that there's more said in Scripture concerning Balaam than there's said about Mary the mother of Jesus. There's more said about him than ten of the apostles of the Lord all put together. Therefore, the Word of God does give some emphasis to him.

The New Testament mentions him three times, always in connection with apostasy. In three of the apocalyptic messages of the New Testament, you will find references to this man. The first is found in 2 Peter 2:15: "Which have forsaken the right way, and are gone astray, following the way of Balaam the son of Bosor, who loved the wages of unrighteousness."

That's the first statement, a warning concerning the "way of Balaam." And then Jude, in his little book, in the eleventh verse, says, "Woe unto them! For they have gone in the way of Cain, and ran greedily after the error of Balaam for reward, and perished in the gainsaying of [Korah]."

Jude warns of the "error of Balaam." The *error* of Balaam and the *way* of Balaam are not the same. Also John, in Revelation, when he gives the prophetic history of the church, goes through that period when the church, a martyr church, stood against the world, then that period when the world like a flood came inside the church. Our Lord's message to that church is in Revelation 2:14: "But I have a few things against thee, because thou hast there them that hold the doctrine of Balaam, who taught Balac to cast a stumbling block before the children of Israel, to eat things sacrificed unto idols, and to commit fornication."

Now here we are told about the "doctrine of Balaam." The *doctrine* of Balaam is different from the *way* of Balaam, and it's different from the *error* of Balaam. Therefore, in attempting to evaluate this man we need to recognize that these three statements give us a character analysis of Balaam. Let's now go back into his history, back into the book of Numbers, to understand these warnings.

As Israel advanced toward the promised land, coming to the end of the forty years of wandering in the wilderness, they entered a new territory. It was the territory of certain nations which were their natural enemies. Israel had gained a victory as they came up against the Ammorites. Naturally, that word had spread so that these nations feared Israel. And when Israel came into the territory of Moab, Balak the king of Moab was afraid to engage them in battle. He resorted to a superstition; that is, he engaged a famous prophet of that day to come and curse Israel. The one that he engaged is the one in whom we're interested, Balaam, the prophet.

Balaam was a Midianite. He was brought from Aram, out of the mountains of the east. And I should say this concerning him: Balaam uttered several of the most wonderful prophecies you'll find in the Word of God. Probably it was on the basis of his prophecy that the wise men came out of the East to Jerusalem asking the question, "Where is he that is born King of the Jews?" (Mt 2:2). So, you see, we can't just dismiss this man and say we can pay no attention to him at all when he gave such an important prophecy as that. Apparently he was a prophet with a very wide reputation in that day because he got results. And the question is, was this man a genuine prophet of God?

Well, let's look at his story, beginning in Numbers 22:6. When the children of Israel came to the east bank of the Jordan River in preparing to cross over into the land God had promised them, naturally Balak, the king of Moab, did not know their intentions. He did not know but what they intended to attack him and wrest his kingdom from him. And therefore, afraid to make an attack upon them but wanting to defend his kingdom, he sent messengers to Balaam. The word that he sent with the messengers was to be this: "Come now therefore, I pray thee, curse for me this people; for they are too mighty for me: perhaps I shall prevail, that we may smite them, and that I may drive them out of the land; for I know that he whom thou blessest is blessed, and he whom thou cursest is cursed" (NSRB).

Now that reveals the reputation Balaam had. Balak sent to him messengers who stated their mission, and they brought with them a very handsome price. "And the elders of Moab and the elders of Midian departed with the rewards of divination in their hand; and they came unto Balaam, and spake unto him the words of Balak" (v. 7). They came to Balaam with a very handsome price for his services, and they said to him, "Balak has sent us and he wants to engage your services. He wants to bring you to curse these people that have recently come up out of Egypt. He has found that they're a dangerous people. So far, they have had victories everywhere they have met the enemy, and he'd like for you to come up."

Well, the very interesting thing is that this man Balaam sounds very genuine. "And he said unto them, Lodge here

this night, and I will bring you word again, as the LORD
shall speak unto me: and the princes of Moab abode with
Balaam" (v. 8). Have you ever heard anything more pious
than that? He sounds genuine, does he not? Balaam
honestly seems to be trying to ascertain the mind of God
here. He said, "If you'll stay here this night, I'll make inquiry of God and see whether I'm to go with you or not."
Well, he did. And he got God's answer.

"And God said unto Balaam, Thou shalt not go with
them; thou shalt not curse the people; for they are blessed"
(v. 12). That's God's final word to Balaam. "You're not
to go, and you're not to curse these people because I have
blessed them." That's God's answer. Now what will be the
reaction of Balaam to that? Here's where, actually, I must
confess that I'm taken off guard.

"And Balaam rose up in the morning and said unto the
princes of Balak, Get you into your land; for the LORD
refuseth to give me leave to go with you" (v. 13). He says,
"I can't go. God has forbidden me to go. I won't go. You
can return to your master and tell him."

"And the princes of Moab rose up, and they went unto
Balak, and said, Balaam refuseth to come with us" (v. 14).
Now if the story ended there, I'd have to say that Balaam
is one of the most remarkable men of God I've ever met.
Here's a man that has a prophecy from God. God gives
him a message, and this man obeys the message. He said,
"No, I won't go." But, unfortunately, the story doesn't end
there. Sometimes we also acquit ourselves in a very fine
way. Don't we? And it's afterward that we have our
difficulty.

Now will you notice that Balak is not going to take no
for an answer. And, candidly, I believe that he knew something about the character of this man Balaam. "And Balak
sent yet again princes, more, and more honourable than
they" (v. 15). It is quite flattering that he now sends some
of the important men of the kingdom to him. "And they
came to Balaam, and said to him, Thus saith Balak the

son of Zippor, Let nothing, I pray thee, hinder thee from coming unto me" (v. 16). They make him a more attractive offer. "For I will promote thee unto very great honour, and I will do whatsoever thou sayest unto me: come therefore, I pray thee, curse me this people" (v. 17).

If I may use the common jargon of the street, Balak upped the ante. He decided to pay him more. Apparently he knew something about Balaam's character. And now listen to this pious prophet. "And Balaam answered and said unto the servants of Balak, If Balak would give me his house full of silver and gold, I cannot go beyond the word of the Lord my God, to do less or more" (v. 18).

Why did he say, "If he gave me a house full of silver and gold"? Because that's what he wanted. Why mention it if you're not thinking about it? "Why," he says, "I wouldn't go even if he gave me a house filled with gold and silver." And when he makes this statement, I can hear a lot of the brethren saying, "Amen. Hallelujah for Balaam. What a testimony he's giving!" But he's not genuine here. He's not telling the truth here. He's going to take a little less than a house filled with gold and silver, but it's going to be a good price. May I say to you, he said this because he was a covetous man. Now listen to him: "Now therefore, I pray you, tarry ye also here this night, that I may know what the Lord will say unto me more" (v. 19).

Why did he say that? He already has God's answer. Why does he say, "Wait here tonight, and I'll go to God again to see if He has changed His mind"? God had said to him, "I don't want you to go, and you're positively *not* to curse these people." That's God's answer. That should be enough. But when you begin to talk about a house filled with silver and gold, it's well to go back and make inquiry again. God may change His mind.

Oh, you've heard the whimsical story of the preacher who came to his wife and said, "I've just gotten a call to the church in the next town. It's a larger town. It's a much better church. The people in it are more refined and cul-

tured, and they do not cause the trouble they do here, and
they've offered me a higher salary. I'm going upstairs and
pray about this to see if it's the Lord's will for me to go."
His wife says, "Fine, I'll go up and pray with you." And
he says, "Oh, my, no. You stay down here and pack up."
Balaam, you see, is going to pray about it some more although he actually has God's answer.

However, it does look like God changes His mind, does
it not? Notice the development here for it's so important.
"And God came unto Balaam at night, and said unto him,
If the men come to call thee, rise up, and go with them; but
yet the word which I shall say unto thee, that shalt thou
do" (v. 20). Now somebody says, "God *did* change His
mind." No, God didn't. You know that there is what is
known as the permissive will of God. There is also the
direct will of God. And there are a great many Christians
today who are taking God's second best or God's third best
because they will not accept the will of God for their lives.
And God permits this. Balaam already had God's mind;
he didn't need to make further inquiry, but there's one
thing sure, a house full of silver and gold is a nice price for
a prophet, and there's no reason why he shouldn't go. So
God permits him to go.

You remember that when the children of Israel com-
plained and murmured in the wilderness to Moses, "We
want something besides manna to eat. We're tired of it.
We want meat." And God says, "I'll give them flesh. I'll
give them flesh till it comes out at their nostrils and they
are sick of it." Later on, the psalmist wrote, "He gave them
their request; but sent leanness into their soul" (Ps
106:15).

There are certain things that you can keep nagging God
about which He'll permit you to do. But, my friend, you'll
dry up spiritually. And there are a great many Christians
that could testify to this experience. Do you want God's
permissive will, or do you want His direct will? Do you
want Him to give you every one of your prayer requests,

or do you really want Him to have His way? Do you want His will to be done, or do you really want God to come over on your side and do what you want done? The interesting thing is there are times when He will do just that.

Now this man Balaam is being permitted to go, but God is going to warn him every step of the way. And He uses something quite interesting. "And Balaam rose up in the morning, and saddled his ass, and went with the princes of Moab. And God's anger was kindled because he went: and the angel of the LORD stood in the way" (Num 22:21-22). And the reason Balaam couldn't see the angel of the Lord was that he was thinking of a house full of silver and gold. He's a covetous man, and he can't see spiritual things. And you talk about a rebuke! God knows how to rebuke. This dumb animal on which he's riding sees the angel; it has more spiritual discernment than he does. My beloved, this is the way of Balaam.

Will you listen to Peter again as he evaluates this man. "Who have forsaken the right way, and are gone astray, following the way of Balaam, the son of Beor, who loved the wages of unrighteousness" (2 Pe 2:15, NSRB).

The minute that prophet left and went with the messengers of Balak he was going astray. He was out of the will of God. He loved the wages of unrighteousness. He was covetous. Listen to Peter in the next verse: "But was rebuked for his iniquity; the dumb ass speaking with man's voice forbad the madness of the prophet." Balaam was thinking, *I just can't wait to get over there and get the job done and get my money.*

My beloved, may I speak very candidly. There are many Christian organizations today that need to be investigated. The way that you measure a Christian organization is whether or not it is after the dollar. That's the way. And some of them won't stand inspection. Some of the most covetous people I've met are in the Lord's work. I've been in this work a quarter of a century, and I've met a great many people. May I say to you, friends, it's always well to investigate and see who's getting rich. Religion can be a racket. And I think every believer is responsible for knowing what he is supporting.

Old Balaam had a message from God, but he was covetous. We're merely on the surface now; let's probe a little deeper. Let's look at the personality of Balaam. Jude tells us this: "Woe unto them! For they have gone in the way of Cain, and ran greedily after the error of Balaam for reward, and perished in the gain-saying of Korah" (Jude 11, NSRB).

Had you met him and said to him, "Now, Brother Balaam, why are you going with these messengers? We understand that God has told you not to go. Why are you going?" Then he would start rationalizing. He could explain his motives, and he could ascribe a worthy motive for his conduct. That's the interesting thing. And there's more pious rationalization today in Christian circles than you can imagine. All of them have a legitimate thrust. A friend of mine said to me, "One of the reasons, McGee, you don't get better support from some of your broadcasts is you just ask people to support a radio program. You need to have some sort of a promotion. You ought to start a home in the Aleutian Islands for stray Maltese cats. There are a lot of people who like cats, and you'll appeal to them, especially if you tell them about how terrible it is for a Maltese cat who's not accustomed to being out in the cold and that you've got a nice warm place for him, provided they'll give to you."

All of these organizations appeal to you on the program that they're reaching this or that group of people. And Christian people somehow or other never stop to see how much the overhead is. I happen to know concerning one organization that for every dollar that's received, eighty percent goes to overhead. Only twenty cents gets to the field where the operation is, although the appeal is always made to the field. No secular business could do that; why, United States Steel couldn't operate like that! My beloved, may I say to you that this fellow Balaam worries us, doesn't he? Here's a man with God's message, but he is rationalizing behind a very pious front.

Look at the scene in the land of Moab. Israel is camping in the valley surrounded by mountains on every side, and the king of the Moabites, Balak, brings Balaam to a mountaintop overlooking the camp. (I do not think that the Israelites knew what was taking place up there.) And he says, "There are the people I'm talking about. I want you to curse them."

Notice Balaam's answer: "How shall I curse whom God hath not cursed? Or how shall I defy whom the LORD hath not defied? For from the top of the rocks I see him, and from the hills I behold him: lo, the people shall dwell alone, and shall not be reckoned among the nations" (Num 23:8-9).

This is one of the greatest prophecies concerning the nation Israel, and it's given through a man who's so covetous he can't see anything but the gold and silver! Balak was dissatisfied, naturally, and he said, "You didn't curse them; you blessed them. Let's go to another mountain peak." He took him around on another side. They went to the top of the mountain, and he said, "Now take a look at them and see if you can curse them."

Now hear Balaam: "Behold, I have received commandment to bless: and he hath blessed; and I cannot reverse it. He hath not beheld iniquity in Jacob, neither hath he seen perverseness in Israel: the LORD, his God, is with him, and the shout of a king is among them" (vv. 20-21).

"I cannot curse them because God does not behold iniquity in Israel." Now how is he rationalizing? Balaam reasoned that God must condemn Israel. Why? Because there was evil in the camp, there was sin in the camp. In other portions we read that there had been rebellion; there had been overt sin, and God had to judge His own people. But, my beloved, will you hear me very carefully. God will deal with His own people, but He's not going to let a

heathen prophet bring an accusation against them. Whom
the Lord has justified no man can condemn. And I say
that's wonderful! The natural man always concludes that
God must judge Israel and judge sinners. That's natural.
I've heard this a dozen times. A vile speaking man, about
ten years ago, said to me after a Thursday night Bible
study, "How can you say that David is a man after God's
own heart when he's a murderer and an adulterer?" I said,
"It is difficult, isn't it? But, brother, it sure ought to en-
courage you and me. If God will take David, maybe He'll
take you and maybe He'll take me." The natural man
knows nothing about imputed righteousness. He knows
nothing about the righteousness that God gives to a condemned sinner when he receives Christ, because Christ
died *for* him on the cross, and He was raised from the dead.
Now that sinner is put in Christ, and God sees him in
Christ.

Paul says: "What shall we then say to these things? If
God be for us, who can be against us? He that spared not
his own Son, but delivered him up for us all, how shall he
not with him also freely give us all things? Who shall lay
anything to the charge of God's elect? It is God that
justifieth" (Ro 8:31-33). Neither can old Balaam, nor any
man today, nor can Satan bring a charge against a sinner
who has turned to Jesus Christ.

"Who is he that condemneth? It is Christ that died, yea
rather, that is risen again, who is even at the right hand of
God, who also maketh intercession for us" (v. 34).

And today, even when Satan, the accuser of the brethren,
steps up and accuses one who is Christ's, the Lord Jesus
Christ says, "I died for him. He is in Me. And You,
Father, can receive him just as You receive Me." Balaam
doesn't know anything about that. That's the error of
Balaam. And that's the error of a great many folk today.

Let's probe a little deeper now by going into the thought
life of Balaam. This brings us to his doctrine. The doctrine of Balaam is satanic; it's demonic; it's hellish; it's

subtle. It's the same thing that appeared in the Garden of Eden to our first parents. In our Lord's message to the church at Pergamum He said, "But I have a few things against thee, because thou hast there them that hold the doctrine of Balaam, who taught Balak to cast a stumbling-block before the children of Israel, to eat things sacrificed unto idols, and to commit fornication" (Rev 2:14).

Balak, you see, found that God would not permit him to curse these people. He realized he would have to adopt a different approach if he's going to get the silver and gold, and that's what he has come for, after all. If you think Balaam is going back empty-handed, you are not acquainted with religious racketeers. Because he wants the rich gifts of Balak, he's going to do something now that's terrible.

"And Israel abode in Shittim, and the people began to commit whoredom with the daughters of Moab" (Num 25:1). As you read this awful account that follows, you will see what has happened as a result of Balaam's counsel. He had said something like this to Balak: "Now I can't curse them, but I can tell you how to destroy them. You go down and join them. Get the good-looking women of Moab to go down to the camp and get acquainted." And so the Moabite women "caused the children of Israel, through the counsel of Balaam, to commit trespass against the LORD" (Num 31:16). With fornication came idolatry into the camp of Israel. What the devil couldn't do by cursing and fighting from the outside, he did from the inside.

Do you know that the Church has never been hurt from the outside? The richest years of the Church were during its persecution. Never has the Church been as rich spiritually, never has it been as evangelistic, never has it reached out to the ends of the earth as it did during those periods. The devil was fighting it from the outside. But he caught on. He couldn't hurt the Church from the outside; so he joined it. Read the story of Constantine. Read about the entrance of all sorts of pagan rituals and rites from the outside. What he couldn't do from the outside he did from within.

There's a great principle here which is applicable to all relationships. Our country, for example, will not, in my opinion, be hurt as a nation from the outside. But I do think we're being destroyed from the inside. It's a great principle. At the present time it is happening to a church I could name. There is not an enemy on the outside that has ever hurt that church, but I know some members who have. A church can be crucified from the inside. That's a principle which Satan has learned.

Let me now make a personal application. Do we understand how God justifies a sinner? Can we say with Paul, "There is now no condemnation to them that are in Christ Jesus"? The death and resurrection of Christ are my hope today, and because these are my hope I stand before God with no condemnation. But that doesn't end the story.

You and I need to search our own motives for conduct and action. Why, really, do you attend church? What is the motive behind your service in the church? Are you seeking applause? Are you seeking power? Perhaps wealth? What's your motive? The difficulty with many of us today is we're acting from mixed motives, and there's frustration in our lives. We're rather like old Balaam. Have you decided whether he's really God's man or not? What kind of a fellow is this that could give these wonderful prophecies of God and talk about his relationship to God, and then do the thing that he did? He was acting from mixed motives, to say the least. Oh, there are so many today that say, "I want to be a Christian, but I want to go just as far into the world as I can."

Although I don't like to close with this kind of a story, I will because it illustrates this principle. The teacher in a class of little boys had given them the story of Lazarus and the rich man. She told about the plight of Lazarus, the beggar. She told about how he suffered down here and what he went through. My, she painted a sad picture. Then she told about the rich man and what he enjoyed. And then she moved over on the other side and told about where the rich man went after death; he went to hades. She told about the poor man who was in Abraham's bosom. That class of little boys was quite solemn. In order to clinch it, she asked, "Which would you rather be, the rich man or Lazarus the beggar?" Well, not one of those little fellows answered. She waited a few moments for it to sink in. Finally, one little fellow put up his hand. He said, "I'd like to be the rich man here and Lazarus hereafter."

There are a lot of Christians like that today. They want to be the rich man here, and the poor man over there, and they think they can do it. If Balaam is in heaven, then they *can* do it. But the Holy Spirit doesn't even tell us. You figure it out. And then I read further on that Balaam was killed by the Israelites (Num 31:8). He was on the wrong side. Balaam, a prophet for profit. What kind of man was he? What kind of a Christian are you today? What kind of Christian am I?

Paul says that we ought to examine ourselves. If you are God's child, you are not under condemnation before Him, and He won't let Satan bring a charge against you, but He Himself will. He'll search your heart and He'll search mine.

I have a letter here from a missionary. I get one to three letters like this every year. It has been a number of years now since I taught at the Bible Institute, but this missionary was a student in my class. She writes, "I cheated, and to this good day" (I don't know how long ago it was, ten years or more), "I can't have my devotionals without that standing in my way." Well, she straightened it out.

You can't get by with sin if you're God's child, for He'll deal with you. But it is confusing to your friends and to those outside. They wonder whether you're genuine or not.

6

THE FORGOTTEN PROPHET
AND A GOD-AIMED
ARROW

Micaiah

1 Kings 22

There is the ever present temptation when we come to the record given in 1 and 2 Kings to emphasize some phase of the life of Elijah. He dominates this area, and his life is rich in interest and in spiritual content. However there is another prophet who is as little known as Elijah is well known. You may not be acquainted with him at all. I want to say this for him: he's in the major league with Elijah. Although he may not be as well known as Elijah, he hit just as many home runs for God as Elijah did.

The difficulty with the prophet we are looking at is that every time he preached a sermon he was put in jail! The reason they put him in jail is that he happened to be the one man standing for God in the courts of Ahab, and what he said was always unfavorable to Ahab. As you know, a great many people do not like to have anything said that is unfavorable to them, and that was true of Ahab, king of Israel.

You will recall in the history of Israel the glorious reign of Solomon, but it concluded with the warning given to him that the kingdom was to be divided. Well, it *was* divided, and there were the ten tribes in the north and the one tribe, Judah (with little Benjamin), in the south. Israel and Judah were to walk their separate ways, but both were to go finally into captivity.

The very interesting thing is that at this particular moment in history we have Ahab, the king of Israel, in the north, and he's the worst king that they ever had—probably the worst king that any kingdom ever had. In contrast, we have in the south Jehoshaphat, king of Judah, and he is one of the very best kings they ever had. Normally, these two kingdoms would have been farther apart than they ever were in their history, but never since they had been separate nations had they been so closely allied. It was an abnormal alliance; it was an unnatural confederacy. The fraternizing of these two kings who were antipathies apart seems strange indeed.

The explanation is not difficult to find. Right down beneath the surface you find that Jehoram, son of Jehoshaphat, king of Judah, had married Athaliah, the daughter of Ahab, king of Israel. (She was to become the bloody Athaliah, killing off all of her grandchildren that she could get her hands on.) Here is a case of where the sons of God and the daughters of men are married again, and of course it wrought havoc. It always will bring havoc at any time under any dispensation at any period in the history of this world, where the sons of God marry the daughters of men, that is, when the saved marry the unsaved.

Now these two men, Ahab and Jehoshaphat, are far apart in their thinking, and in their relationship to God; yet you find them joining up.

Ahab had Jehoshaphat over for a visit. They're kinfolk now anyway, so it was natural to get together for a visit. And while he was there—Ahab evidently had planned this—he arranged to say at a particular moment, "We have lost Ramoth-gilead to the king of Syria. It's necessary for us to go and get it, and I'm just wondering, Jehoshaphat, if you'd like to join with me in going and rescuing this part of our nation. After all, you're part of the family and you're part of the nation also. Would you join with me?"

Lo and behold, Jehoshaphat agrees to it. He says, "Yes, I'll be perfectly willing to join with you."

Now this man Jehoshaphat was God's man. As we see in the book of Chronicles, one of the five revival periods took place during his reign. He had a heart for God, and he wanted to do the will of God, which is evident in the request he makes: "And Jehoshaphat said unto the king of Israel, Enquire, I pray thee, at the word of the Lord to day" (1 Ki 22:5). In other words, he said, "I'll be glad to join with you, but I want to know what God's will is in the matter. I'm wondering if you wouldn't get the prophets in and let's find out what the will of God is."

So this man Ahab had the paid preachers of the day trotted in. "Then the king of Israel gathered the prophets together, about four hundred men, and said unto them, Shall I go against Ramoth-gilead to battle, or shall I forbear? And they said, Go up; for the Lord shall deliver it into the hand of the king" (v. 6). They are saying, you see, the thing that Ahab wanted to hear.

This has always been a great danger, and is, of course, the place to which the pulpit in America has come. As someone has said, the pulpit in America has become a sounding board instead of the voice in the wilderness crying out for God. It is saying the thing that people want to hear today. That is the tragedy of this hour in which we live.

These prophets, who all eat at the table of Ahab, know which side their bread is buttered on, and so they say the thing that Ahab wants to hear. They say, "Go on up to battle. You'll win."

Now this man Jehoshaphat is God's man, and he has spiritual discernment. He knows that these four hundred prophets are not giving God's message. "And Jehoshaphat said, Is there not here a prophet of the Lord besides, that we might inquire of him?" (v. 7). Jehoshaphat is wondering, "Couldn't we get a really spiritually minded prophet that has the mind of the Lord and has the courage to declare it? Don't you have a man like that?"

"And the king of Israel said unto Jehoshaphat, There is yet one man, Micaiah the son of Imlah, by whom we may enquire of the LORD" (v. 8). Thank God for the one man, but what a tragic hour. "There is yet *one* man." There are four hundred who are willing to please, and *one* man willing to stand for God. There is yet one man—and he names him—he is Micaiah. (He's probably the only Jewish Scotsman there is in the Bible! It ought to be MacCaiah, as you can see. He's a Scotsman.)

Now here is his introduction. They've had dinner together, you remember, and now Ahab is introducing, as it were, their after-dinner speaker. How would you like an introduction like this? "But I hate him." Ahab said, "Yes, there is one prophet here in the kingdom who speaks for the Lord, but I hate him." And I tell you, the man who gives God's Word will come in under the lash, the tongue-lashing, of those who do not want the Word of God today.

"But I hate him; for he doth not prophesy good concerning me, but evil." You hear some people say today, "When I go to church, I want to be comforted." I heard of a man who left a church that I was pastoring for the reason that he wasn't being comforted. If what they tell me about his business is true, he doesn't need comfort, he needs to be rebuked. May I say to you, my friends, in this hour we probably need something other than comforting words in America. Our nation has come to a place where people do not want to hear the things which have to do with sin, the things which rebuke them within. They do not want the Word of God really turned upon their souls and upon their hearts and upon their lives.

So Ahab says, "I hate him." And actually that is the best compliment that Micaiah ever had. I heard some time ago a famous preacher in America say this, "I do not judge a man by the friends that he has. I judge him by the enemies that he makes. And if he has the right enemies, he's the right kind of man." We are known today not only by the friends we keep but also we're known by the enemies that we make. I heard of a man the other day at whose funeral service the preacher said, "This man did not have an enemy." Well, when I was told that, I said, "I did not know that Mr. Milquetoast had died." He is the only one who could die without having an enemy. The best thing that you could say for Micaiah was that Ahab hated him. If Ahab had loved him, there would have been something wrong with Micaiah.

In our day there is a notion being circulated throughout America, and it's being called Christianity, that we're to love everything and that we're to love everybody. Even the secular press has had to call attention to the fact that America has lost its moral consciousness. Even the church has lost its conscience in America today, and has no moral courage whatsoever.

I love this fellow Micaiah. In this day of compromise, it is wonderful to see a man like this. In a day when it's peace at any price, in a day when men are compromising in every field, especially in politics and religion, it's wonderful to see this man stand out for God. And this is the man we're considering now, this forgotten prophet, Micaiah, who apparently spent most of his active ministry in jail. He would come out and give a message and back to jail he would go. And that's where he was when he was summoned to appear before Ahab and Jehoshaphat.

Actually, Micaiah was the best friend Ahab ever had. If he had only listened to Micaiah, his life would have been spared, he would not have been killed in battle. But he did not listen. It reminds me of what Paul said to the Galatians (4:16): "Am I therefore become your enemy, because I tell you the truth?" Why, Micaiah was the *friend* of Ahab.

Now will you notice this dramatic scene that is before

us. To me this is one of the richest scenes you will find in the Word of God.

"And the king of Israel and Jehoshaphat, the king of Judah, sat each on his throne, having put on their robes, in a threshing floor at the entrance of the gate of Samaria, and all the prophets prophesied before them" (1 Ki 22:10, NSRB). Here are these two sovereigns. One sits upon the throne of Judah, and the other sits upon the throne of Israel. Before them are four hundred prophets, the boys who are paid to say the nice things, going around smiling and saying to Ahab, "Go up, go up. You will win the battle. Everything will be in your favor. You go right ahead and do this." That's the scene.

Jehoshaphat, however, is puzzled. He is not satisfied with what these paid preachers are saying. A guard is sent over now to get Micaiah who is in jail. They keep him handy. They always know where he is when they do want a word from God.

On the way back the messenger says to him, "Now look here, Micaiah, you're just a killjoy here at this court, and you never say anything that puts you in good standing with Ahab. I suggest that you go ahead and agree with the prophets. They've all told the king to go against Ramoth-gilead and God would give it to him. If you'll just join in the chorus there loud and lustily, it will put you in favor, and we won't have to bring you back to jail again." Listen to Micaiah: "And Micaiah said, As the LORD liveth, what the LORD saith unto me, that will I speak" (v. 14).

Now Micaiah comes in. These 400 prophets are milling around, the two kings are sitting on their thrones, Jehoshaphat is a little puzzled, and Ahab says, "Micaiah, shall we go against Ramoth-gilead to battle, or shall we forbear?" (v. 15).

Now here is a man with a sense of humor. God has a sense of humor, friend, and His Word is filled with it. Here is an example. Micaiah looks about and sees what is going on; so he mimics the prophets. "And he answered him, Go, and prosper: for the LORD shall deliver it into the hand of the king." And I think he begins to trot around with the other prophets.

Now Ahab knows this fellow, and he knows he is pulling his leg. He knows he has not yet given the message from God. "And the king said unto him, how many times shall I adjure thee that thou tell me nothing but that which is true in the name of the LORD?" (v. 16). "Quit kidding me, Micaiah. What is the message?"

Now Micaiah becomes serious and he gives God's message. Listen to it: "And he said, I saw all Israel scattered upon the hills, as sheep that have not a shepherd: and the LORD said, These have no master: let them return every man to his house in peace" (v. 17). It means that Ahab will be killed in battle: he, of course, is the master of his people.

You would think that Ahab would receive this message and thank the prophet for giving him a word that would have spared his life. He should have been grateful to him. But notice his reaction: "And the king of Israel said unto Jehoshaphat, Did I not tell thee that he would prophesy no good concerning me, but evil?" (v. 18). "He never says anything good to me. He always says things that are bad to me, and I don't like it. I hate him!" That's Ahab. Micaiah was the only one there who *did* know the truth and the only one there giving the truth.

Now he does something that is, without doubt, the most masterly thing you'll find in the entire Word of God. It was a dramatic scene before, but it becomes doubly dramatic now. This man Micaiah uses satire, biting satire. He uses the rapier of ridicule, and it's devastating. Listen to him as he gives this word that all Israel is to be scattered and Ahab is to be killed. Poor old Ahab had just said, "I told you so. That's the thing he always says—bad news for me." Now Micaiah gives a parable. (You remember that our Lord turned to parables only when the people would not hear. Parables are for folk who will not hear God's Word. It is the way to elicit their interest and to at least get the message to them.)

Micaiah gives a preposterous parable, and it's one of these parables by contrast. As you know, a parable is given to illustrate truth. In fact, the word *parable* is in the Greek *balo,* meaning "to throw" and *para,* meaning "by the side of." It means to throw or put down by the side of a thing something else to measure it. If you put a yardstick down beside the desk in front of me, that's a parable. It tells you how long it is. And so a parable is something that is put down by the side of something to illustrate it. But at times it illustrates by contrast. You remember that the Lord Jesus gave parables like that. When the religious rulers began to turn from Him, He gave the parable of the unjust judge. He said that there was a widow who camped on his doorstep, and the unjust judge did not want to hear her case because she had no political power nor did she carry any vote in his community. But she stayed there and stayed there and stayed there some more until he had to hear her to get rid of her. Now do you think that God is an unjust judge, and that you have to camp on His doorstep, that you have to plead and beg Him to do something for you? No. He is the opposite. It is a parable by contrast, you see.

Now notice the parable that Micaiah gives. I wish I could have seen him as he gave it. I'm confident there was a gleam in his eye, and a wry smile on his face. Here it is:

"And he said, Hear thou, therefore, the word of the LORD. I saw the LORD sitting on his throne, and all the host of heaven standing by him on his right hand and on his left" (v. 19). In other words, there is a special "board of directors" meeting called in heaven, with God as the Chairman of the board.

"And the LORD said, Who shall persuade Ahab, that he may go up and fall at Ramoth-gilead? And one said on this manner, and another said on that manner" (v. 20).

Isn't that ridiculous? Imagine God calling a meeting of the board of directors in heaven and saying, "Now I've called you together in order to get some advice. A problem has come up that is too big for Me to handle. Ahab is to go to battle and be killed, but how in the world will I get him into battle? I just don't know what to do." And one spirit got up and said, "I think this." And the rest shook their heads and said, "No, that doesn't sound good." Another spirit got up and said something else. Everybody shook their heads and said, "No, we won't do that either." Finally one little spirit stood up with a suggestion that sounded like a good one. I wish I had been there to ask Micaiah how a spirit stands! But he was smiling all the time he was giving this, you see. I like the way Micaiah tells it: "And there came forth a spirit, and stood before the LORD, and said, I will persuade him" (v. 21).

My friend, can you imagine God asking for advice? It is utterly ridiculous. Notice Isaiah 40:13: "Who hath directed the Spirit of the LORD, or being his counselor hath taught him?" God hasn't been to school; no one has taught Him. God never asks anybody for advice. The apostle Paul exclaimed in Romans 11:33-34, "O the depth of the riches both of the wisdom and knowledge of God! How unsearchable are his judgments, and his ways past finding out! For who hath known the mind of the Lord? or who hath been his counsellor?"

Have you ever noticed that when our Lord Jesus Christ was down here in the flesh, there were two things He never did? He never did appeal to His own mind as being the final place of decision for any action that He took. He never said to anyone, "I'm going to do this because I've been thinking about it all night and I've come to the conclusion it's the best thing to do." Every time He did something he said, "This is my Father's will. I've come to do my Father's will." He never appealed to His own mind even when He was a man. And then the second thing, He never asked anyone for advice. He never called together

His disciples and said, "Now, fellows, I'm in a quandary. Shall I go to Jerusalem or shall I stay here?" Never did He ask them that. (There was one exception, I grant you, at the feeding of the 5,000. He turned to Philip and asked, "Whence shall we buy bread?" But the gospel writer hastens to add, "And this he said to prove him: for he himself knew what he would do." The Lord Jesus never asked anybody for advice.

Oh, today, my friend, God is not asking for advice. And down here He doesn't need our advice. How many fine Christian organizations and movements that were started by godly men led of God have fallen into the hands of unspiritual men who are determined to have their way and are riding through roughshod over the hearts and lives of multitudes! Oh, my friend, your way is not better than God's way! God doesn't want your advice. He is not asking how to run His business. He is telling you and me what to do. God does not need advice!

However, Micaiah has Him in a board of directors meeting where He is puzzled and is getting information. Now Micaiah makes his point: "And there came forth a spirit, and stood before the Lord, and said, I will persuade him. And the Lord said unto him, Wherewith? And he said, I will go forth, and I will be a lying spirit in the mouth of all his prophets. And he said, Thou shalt persuade him, and prevail also: go forth, and do so. Now, therefore, behold, the Lord hath put a lying spirit in the mouth of all these thy prophets, and the Lord hath spoken evil concerning thee" (1 Ki 22:21-23).

This is sparkling, striking, and startling satire. I do not know of a better way of calling the crowd of prophets there a bunch of liars than to tell this little story. That's exactly what Micaiah is doing. He says that this spirit came from God as a lying spirit in the mouth of these false prophets.

Now Ahab doesn't like it, of course. He wants to get rid of Micaiah. "And the king of Israel said, Take Micaiah, and carry him back unto Amon the governor of the city, and to Joash the king's son; and say, Thus saith the king, Put this fellow in the prison, and feed him with bread of affliction and with water of affliction, until I come in peace" (vv. 26-27). In other words, "Wait until I get back from the battle. I'll take care of him for talking to me like that!"

But Micaiah had the last word: "And Micaiah said, If thou return at all in peace, the LORD hath not spoken by me. And he said, Hearken, O people, every one of you" (v. 28).

In effect he said, "Listen. If you even come back here, Ahab, the Lord hasn't spoken by me. And I don't care about your hearing it because you're not coming back, but I want these other people to hear it so they will know I was speaking God's word to you."

Well, the armies of Ahab and Jehoshaphat go to battle against the king of Assyria. This man Ahab has a bag filled with tricks. He has persuaded Jehoshaphat to go into the battle on his side, and knowing the king of Syria is after him, he says to Jehoshaphat, "You keep on your king's robes, but I'll change into a regular buck private's outfit." And he does that. It is a perfect disguise. There is not a way in the world for the king of Syria to know who Ahab is. The battle is joined, and, I tell you, it is fortunate that Jehoshaphat is not killed in battle. He is almost taken, but he escapes by the skin of his teeth, and he returns like a whipped dog licking his wounds.

For awhile, it looks as if Ahab will escape like the slippery eel that he is. It looks as if Providence is on his side, that the prophecy is wrong and Micaiah is to be confused and God mocked. But then something happens.

One fellow in the infantry, equipped with bow and arrows, has one arrow left. *Well,* he thinks, *no use keeping it. I want my sergeant to think I was busy shooting the enemy so I'll get rid of this one.* The record puts it this way: "And a certain man drew a bow at a venture" (v. 34). He just pulled it. He didn't aim at Ahab. King Ahab had on a regular soldier's uniform; nobody knew who he was.

And this soldier just pulls his bow at a venture, and lets the arrow fly. But that arrow has Ahab's name on it, and God had written it there.

My friend, we've heard a great deal about guided missiles in our day. This is a guided missile, and probably the first one. God was guiding this missile, and it reached its destination. It was a God-aimed arrow, and it found its way between the joints of the armor of Ahab, and found its way to his heart. He was mortally wounded. He told his charioteer to take him out of battle, that he had been hit.

"And the battle increased that day; and the king was held up in his chariot against the Syrians, and died at evening, and the blood ran out of the wound into the inside of the chariot. . . . So the king died, and was brought to Samaria; and they buried the king in Samaria. And one washed the chariot in the pool of Samaria, and the dogs licked up his blood; and they washed his armor, according unto the word of the LORD which he spoke" (vv. 35, 37-38, NSRB).

God, through Elijah, had already told Ahab (after he had caused the death of Naboth so he could seize his property) this: "In the place where dogs licked the blood of Naboth shall dogs lick thy blood, even thine" (21:19). So the body of the king of Israel was brought back to Samaria. And they washed the chariot of his blood, and the dogs licked it, just as God said it would come to pass—literally fulfilled.

Now Ahab's death probably was listed in the paper as being totally accidental, but in God's record it was providential.

And today, without any apology at all, may I say that God is still using that method. And God never misses. The psalmist says, "But God shall shoot at them with an arrow; suddenly shall they be wounded" (Ps 64:7). There is many a man today going through this world who says, "I've escaped so far. Everything that has happened to me has been good. I do not have to answer to God." I say to you this day, there is an arrow that has already been shot from the bow of heaven with his name on it, and that arrow is the arrow of judgment when we will stand before Almighty God.

Sometimes even God's own have an arrow shot at them. You remember the thing that Job said: "For the arrows of the Almighty are within me" (Job 6:4). Job found, even as God's man, that sometimes God wounds one of His own and brings him down to humble him.

But, my beloved, when the arrow of my sin was aimed, it went into Christ Jesus. Someone has said that we entered the heart of Christ through a spear wound. And the arrow of my sin wounded Him. The arrow of my sin put Him to death. Isaiah expresses it this way: "But he was wounded for our transgressions, he was bruised for our iniquities: . . . it pleased the LORD to bruise him; he hath put him to grief" (Is 53:5, 10). He stepped in front of the arrow of God's judgment that was intended for you and me in order that we might not come into judgment. We are passed from judgment unto life.

And now the psalmist says something else. "Thou shalt not be afraid for the terror by night; nor for the arrow that flieth by day" (Ps 91:5). That arrow that is flying by day is the arrow that's aimed at my sin. It has already found its mark in Christ. Therefore I need not be afraid of the arrow that flieth by day.

Right now your sin is either on you or it's on Christ. If you, by faith, receive Him, then He bears that sin for you; He becomes your Saviour, and you will never have to come into judgment, but you're passed from death unto life. The arrows of God's judgment fell upon Him.

7

A DATE WITH DANGER AND DESTINY AT DOTHAN

Elisha

Genesis 37:13-28; 2 Kings 6:8-17

There are three miracle periods in the Bible, and they cluster around personalities. The first miracle period was during the time of Moses and Joshua—all the way from the burning bush to the burning sun. The bush was not consumed, and the sun did not move. I do not mean that there were not miracles before that, but Abraham, Isaac, and Jacob were not miracle workers. This is the first great miracle period.

Then the second great miracle period took place during the time of Elijah and Elisha, which ushered in the era of the prophets and their line.

Then the third miracle period begins in the New Testament with Jesus and His apostles. John the Baptist was not a miracle worker. In fact, the Scriptures specifically state in John 10:41, "John did no miracle." And I do not mean to imply by this that there were no miracles before these periods or after these periods or between these periods, but miracles were the exception and not the rule, you will find that they were sparse and scarce. However during these three periods, miracles abounded.

Now we want to move into the orbit of one of these

miracle periods, the time of Elijah and Elisha. And it is in this period that we shall see Elisha performing more miracles than Elijah did. I grant you that Elijah was more spectacular and more dramatic, but the miracles of Elisha far exceeded those of Elijah. And, after all, that is the way it should have been because we are told that a double portion of the spirit of Elijah came upon Elisha.

Now the incident that is before us begins like this in 2 Kings 6:8, "Then the king of Syria warred against Israel." It sounds very much up to date, does it not? They have been at it for a long time, and actually, it was an old conflict even at that time. The present conflict between Israel and the Arab world has a definite Bible background.

Now notice the situation, as recorded in 2 Kings 6:8-11:

"Then the king of Syria warred against Israel, and took counsel with his servants, saying, In such and such a place shall be my camp. And the man of God sent unto the king of Israel, saying, Beware that thou pass not such a place; for there the Syrians are come down. And the king of Israel sent to the place which the man of God told him and warned him of, and saved himself there, not once nor twice. Therefore, the heart of the king of Syria was sore troubled for this thing; and he called his servants, and said unto them, Will ye not show me which of us is for the king of Israel?"

The king of Syria was disturbed because every plan he made and every place he went was discovered by the king of Israel. He came to the conclusion that there was a spy in his camp. He called together his military and attempted to ferret out the traitor. "Which one of you is for the king of Israel?" Honestly there was no one; all of them were loyal to him.

"And one of his servants said, None, my lord, O king: but Elisha, the prophet that is in Israel, telleth the king of Israel the words that thou speakest in thy bedchamber" (v. 12). The prophet Elisha had "bugged" even the bedroom of the king of Syria and knew everything he said.

And the way he bugged them in that day was that the Lord revealed this to him.

So the king of Syria decided to eliminate Elisha. He first sent out those to spy out where he was, and they located him in Dothan. Dothan is a place north of Jerusalem about sixty miles. It means "two wells" and was a place where there was good pasture, a place where flocks were brought. I am told it never was a very prominent place. But it was the headquarters of Elisha at this particular time.

The king of Syria sends in the military, and they entirely surround the place. The servant of Elisha goes out in the morning, I suppose to get water out of one of those wells (which are still there today). He looks around and sees that the city of Dothan is surrounded by the hosts of Syria. You can be sure of one thing: he is alarmed. He comes back and reports to Elisha, and he says to him, "Alas my master! What shall we do? The city is surrounded. We might just as well give up. It looks hopeless for us! What can we do under these circumstances?"

Elisha says this to him: "Fear not: for they that be with us are more than they that be with them" (v. 16). And I want to tell you that seemed rather unrealistic because here were the hosts of Syria outside, and Elisha is very much alone with his servant, and that servant is frightened to death. So Elisha prays, and his prayer is interesting. "I pray thee, open his eyes, that he may see. And the LORD opened the eyes of the young man; and he saw: and, behold, the mountain was full of horses and chariots of fire round about Elisha" (v. 17). May I say to you that these are still about the children of God, and have always been about them. We don't see them: that is our difficulty today. We feel very much alone too many times.

But this is the kind of story in the Bible that thrills a great many of the saints. It is wonderful to read that the mountain was full of horses and chariots of fire round about Elisha, and we need not fear, for they who are for us

are greater than those who are for the other side. Hallelujah!

And those who like to shout "Hallelujah" in an emotional way, can cite other thrilling instances in Scripture.
Take Israel at the Red Sea: what a miraculous and marvelous deliverance was wrought there! And remember that
God put a hedge about Job so Satan could not touch him.
Also David went out and slew the giant Goliath. Daniel
spent a night in the den of lions and he was unharmed.
Paul was shipwrecked, but the entire crew and passenger
list were all saved. Peter was in prison, and the doors
opened to him of their own accord, and he walked out of
the prison free. How wonderful! Hallelujah!

The question now arises: Is this the stated policy of God
in dealing with His own? Is this a mathematical axiom
that we can follow today? Is it a fixed formula? Is it a
scientific law that we can go by? Is it a set rule? Is it a
sure method of God in dealing with His own?

Well, I have discovered that a great many Christians
today have become great escape artists. They are sort of
spiritual Houdinis. They can tell you about miraculous
instances of God delivering them and leading them. But
many other saints have to bow their heads in shame and
say, "I've had no such experience, and I have had no such
leading from God. It must mean that either I am out of
touch with Him, or He is not for me at all." My friend,
let's go back to Dothan. The answer, I believe, is here.
Dothan is mentioned only two times in the Bible, and
I think for a definite reason.

Another man approaches Dothan, a young man. In fact,
he is a boy seventeen years of age, and danger and destiny
await him there. Actually he is walking like a helpless
and unsuspecting animal into a trap, and I feel like warning him, "Don't go to Dothan!" But that foolish "Hou-
dini" Christian I referred to is apt to say, "You don't need
to worry, preacher. No harm is going to come to him. He's
not going to be hurt at Dothan. He will be home next week

because God will deliver him. After all, there are chariots of fire around Dothan, and he will be delivered." But is he? Joseph's brothers conspire against him. They want to murder him, and after they cool off just a little, the wiser of the brothers recommends that he be sold into slavery. My friend, that was worse than death in that day. It was a living hell to be sold into slavery; yet that is what is happening to this boy, seventeen years of age, and he happens to be God's man! Where are the chariots of fire? That is the skeptic's question. I thought you said that God would deliver him, and He did not. There's no miracle at Dothan.

Gideon had the same question, "Where are the miracles that our fathers told us about?" Gideon is one of the biggest skeptics you will meet in the Word of God. When the angel appears to him, he said, "Don't talk to me. Where are these miracles that our fathers told us about when we came out of Egypt? Look at us today! We are under the Midianites."

I must say this, foolish Christian, you are wrong. You are dead wrong. There are chariots of fire there, but they operate differently. Mr. Skeptic, you are wrong also. Just because you cannot see the chariots of fire does not mean they are not there. They are there. I see more evidences of the hand of God in the life of Joseph than I see in the life of Elisha who performed miracles, yet God never appeared to Joseph, never performed a miracle for him. But I see that God used this seeming disaster and Joseph recognized it later on at the end of his life. He could say to his brothers, "Ye thought evil against me; but God meant it unto good."

And at Dothan the chariots of fire are there, but they are going to be used in a different way. They will let Joseph go into slavery because God is going to use this method to get the children of Israel out from the land of Canaan. The Canaanites were an abomination in that day, living in the grossest immorality, wracked with venereal disease. Read the story of Judah, and you see how the

family of Jacob was already sinking. God got them out of
there, and put them in a different environment. He chose
the land of Goshen down yonder in Egypt to separate
them, to make them a nation, and He is going to use
Joseph to do it. And so the chariots of fire are there to lead
him to Egypt and later on to get the children of Israel
there.

God does not lead all His children in the same path. He
is not pouring every Christian into the same mold. He
does not want, apparently, assembly-line believers. He is
not making Fords, He is making the faithful. He is not
making Chevrolets; He is making Christians. He is not
making transistors; He is transforming people! And so the
experience will be different for each one. Not even two
fingerprints are alike today. God made us that way, for we
are different. It is amazing what God can do with two ears,
two eyes, one nose, and one mouth. He sure comes up with
some funny designs. And if you don't believe it, look
around you. No two are alike. He makes everyone different.

Now do not expect Him to deal with you as He has
dealt with someone else. One believer's life is not a pattern by which to cut another. There is an oversimplification
of the Christian life today. One Christian says, "This is
the way God did it for me." Well, thank God He did it for
you that way, but do not expect Him to do it exactly that
way for me. God will not perform a miracle for you if
there is another way to accomplish His purpose. And if He
does perform a miracle in your life, it does not mean He
will perform it in the life of another believer the same way.

Observe this, my emotional friend, Satan could not get
through the hedge that was around Job, but God let him
through. David, though he slew a giant, was driven from
Jerusalem by Absalom, his own son. While it is true that
Daniel could spend a night in a den of lions and not be
hurt, he died in a pagan court. It is true that Paul was
delivered in a shipwreck, but he was beheaded in Rome.

It is true that Peter walked out of prison, but later on he was crucified. You see, friend, there are some pertinent and practical principles for us here in our Dothan. There is always danger and destiny at Dothan for every person, and you and I will come to this place sooner or later.

From the obvious lessons to be learned at Dothan, I would like to mention five.

First of all, we cannot pattern our lives after others. Two men approach Dothan. One of them endures a fate worse than death. The other is miraculously delivered. Chronologically the instance concerning Joseph took place first. If one life is to be patterned after another, I can well imagine Elisha saying to his servant, "I'm sorry, boy, but we're going to have to give up because one of my ancestors by the name of Joseph was sold into slavery here. It looks like we go to Syria." Oh, no. That will not be the way. Elisha can expect to be delivered, but not Joseph, because there are two situations, and these are two different men. There is a purpose of God in the life of each one, and all of this must be taken into consideration.

There is another illustration of this, and I always have to smile when I read this over in the eighth chapter of Ezra. You will recall that Ezra was a priest; Nehemiah was a layman; in fact, he was an official in the Persian court. When he went up to Jerusalem as an official of the court, taking a leave of absence, he asked for practically the entire army of Persia to see him up there and to protect him. And he had a perfect right to do it. There is no lack of faith on his part for doing this. But, you see, Ezra is different. He is God's priest, and this is what he says, "Then I proclaimed a fast there, at the river of Ahava, that we might afflict ourselves before our God, to seek of him a right way for us, and for our little ones, and for all our substance. For I was ashamed to require of the king a band of soldiers and horsemen to help us against the enemy in the way: because we had spoken unto the king, saying, The hand of our God is upon all them for good who

seek him; but his power and his wrath are against all them
who forsake him. So we fasted and besought our God for
this: and he was intreated of us" (Ezra 8:21-23).

Ezra said, "As a priest, I went into the presence of the
king, and I asked the king to let us go, and I waxed elo-
quent, and I said to the king, 'God is on our side. He will
see us through, and He is against our enemies.' Now I
would feel pretty foolish going back to the king and saying,
'Would you let me have a detachment of soldiers to go
along and protect me?' And the king would say, 'I thought
you were trusting the Lord.' " Ezra said, "I couldn't go
back, and I turned to God and I explained to Him my circumstances, and God brought us up without any protection." But Nehemiah had the whole army back of him!
God uses different methods in dealing with His own.

Years ago a man by the name of George Muller opened
a home for orphans in England. Without any financial
backing and in complete dependence upon God alone, he
fed, clothed, and housed two thousand orphans year by
year. Many times there was not food enough for the next
meal, but God provided it in time. A great many people
read that story, and they said, "This is great! This is the
way it should be done." And so they started orphans'
homes. And do you know that a great many orphans almost starved to death because God had led George Muller
in this way. You see, He had not led these others, they
were merely imitating George Muller.

A businessman in Los Angeles told me of his bitter
experience. He said, "I heard a man say that God was his
partner in business. I was making money, and I thought,
'My, this is great. I'll take God as my partner, and I'll
make more money.' " Then he said, "I took Him on as
partner, and I went bankrupt! I felt like God let me
down." Well, I said, "God led the other man, but He
didn't lead you. You were imitating the other man. You
wanted to make money. The other man apparently was
trying to glorify God." How many people today think

that because God leads one person one way, they can fall in step.

Now I know that someone is thinking of Scriptures like Philippians 3:17, where Paul says, "Brethren, be followers together of me, and mark them which walk so as ye have us for an ensample." And then over in Philippians 4:9 he says, "Those things, which ye have both learned, and received, and heard, and seen in me, do: and the God of peace shall be with you." But Paul here is talking about his conduct. As believers we are to have the same *motives,* but we are in situations that differ and that calls for a different approach to the situation. Therefore, we cannot always pattern our lives after other Christians.

The second great principle revealed here is this: we cannot insist that others pattern their lives after ours. Two men approach Dothan. It is the place of danger and destiny. One is not an example for the other. And our lives are not a norm for others. Many Christians today, because they got saved a certain way, feel that everybody ought to be saved in the same way. But people are saved in different ways, by different methods, by different means. And you cannot put everybody in the same mold, my beloved. God uses different methods.

I think of the old fable of the opossum that lost his tail. He was a little embarrassed because of it. He backed up against a tree and called a meeting of all the other animals and suggested that all of them cut off their tails. One of them edged around behind him and got a look. When they found out what had happened, they decided that they wouldn't follow the same way. That is only a fable, but I have heard Christians who want everybody to fall in and do it the same way they do it. That is not God's method, friend.

And we find that even the Lord Jesus had to rebuke one of his men for this. You will recall that when the Lord Jesus told Simon Peter what was going to happen to him, he had to get nosey and wanted to know what was going to happen to John. "Peter seeing him saith to Jesus, Lord, and what shall this man do?" (Jn 21:21). His thought seemed to be, "Since I'm to be crucified, I guess John ought to be crucified too." "Jesus saith unto him, If I will that he tarry till I come, what is that to thee? Follow thou me" (Jn 21:22). He will deal differently with John. John lived to be about one hundred years old; Simon Peter didn't make it; he was crucified. God deals with folk differently.

Then there is a third great principle that is revealed here. The lack of deliverance is not to be interpreted as the disfavor of God. Two men approach Dothan. It is danger and destiny for both of them. One is delivered; one is sold into slavery. Are we to conclude that God does not love poor Joseph because He let him be sold into slavery, and the chariots of fire were not there to deliver him? Oh, no, my beloved. The chariots of fire were there, but they are not there to do what Joseph wanted done. They are there to accomplish God's purpose, not our whim.

Another illustration of this is found in the New Testament. You will recall the wave of persecution that broke upon the early church: "Now about that time Herod the king stretched forth his hands to vex certain of the church. And he killed James the brother of John with the sword. And because he saw it pleased the Jews, he proceeded further to take Peter also" (Ac 12:1-3). Peter is put in prison. James is killed. Peter escapes death by God's direct intervention. Is God playing favorites? Oh, no. That is the way He deals with us.

One of the great missionaries to India was the man who is probably responsible on the human plane for this modern mission period in which we live today—William Carey, the cobbler; another was a very wonderful young man mentally, morally and every way, who would have had a brilliant career in business—Henry Martyn. His story is a thrill to me. William Carey went to India, did a tremendous work, opened up India for missions, lived out his days. Henry Martyn went out, began a brilliant work, took sick, and died while he was still a young man. Why did God not let *him* live out his life? Well, I don't know the exact reason. The only thing I know is that there is a great principle involved in this life: God is accomplishing His purposes in the world, and to accomplish that purpose He deals differently with those who are His own. Carey will stay and live out his life. Martyn will have to die with his work just begun. That is God's method, and it is not our business to question.

I mention a fourth. This places a compulsion and a restraint upon us to walk at all times in fellowship with God. Both men, Joseph and Elisha, were in fellowship with God at Dothan. However, there are other men who got into trouble because they were out of fellowship. I see them going to Dothan, only it is spelled differently. Abraham goes into Egypt. He is definitely out of the will of God and he acquires in Egypt something he never should have gotten. When I see on television Syrian representatives next to Israeli representatives, I am reminded that they are brothers, but how they hate each other! It is too bad that Abraham went down to Egypt.

There is danger and destiny at Dothan. We need to stay in the will of God. David goes to the housetop when he should have been on the field of battle with his men. That's his Dothan. Jonah goes down and buys a ticket to Dothan; only it is spelled *T-a-r-s-h-i-s-h* in his case. There is danger and destiny at Dothan.

A young man sat in my study and wept as he told me his story. He had come to California for a brief period of six months, got out of the will of God, and married an unsaved woman. That's when he started having trouble. Today there is danger and destiny at Dothan. How important it is to stay in the will of God!

I should like to make this practical and personal. You and I have a date at Dothan. For us it is spelled differently, but there is danger and destiny there. The chariots of fire are about you and me. Oh, I know you have not seen them, and the skeptic laughs and ridicules them, but they are there. You ask, "How do you know?" Because John says, "Greater is he that is in you, than he that is in the world" (1 Jn 4:4). What a comfort! At this moment you may be facing a decision. You have a problem. You have a burden. You have a sorrow. You have a temptation. There is danger and destiny at Dothan. It was Brutus whom Shakespeare had say,

> There is a tide in the affairs of men,
> Which, taken at the flood, leads on to fortune,
> Omitted, all the voyage of their life
> Is bound in shallows and in miseries.

Oh, I tell you, when you and I come to our Dothan, we had better be in fellowship with God, or we may find the angels and the chariots of fire are not effective for us in any way. We need that fellowship.

John, in his first epistle, says, "And these things write we unto you, that your joy may be full" (1 Jn 1:4). The Lord wants you to have a good time, but He also says that it depends on your fellowship with Him. "If we say that we have fellowship with him, and walk in darkness, we lie, and do not the truth: but if we walk in the light, as he is in the light, we have fellowship one with another, and the blood of Jesus Christ, his Son, cleanseth us from all sin" (1 Jn 1:6-7).

There is just one other principle that I see at Dothan. I see another man coming to Dothan, only for Him it is spelled *C-a-l-v-a-r-y*, and sometimes *G-o-l-g-o-t-h-a*. I see Christ coming to the cross! And even the apostles, for they were scattered, said, "He *cannot* die on the cross. He must come down." But I read, "He that spared not his own Son, but delivered him up for us all—" The Father did not spare Him. When Jesus Christ came to His Dothan, He died. But He died, my friend, so that you and I can have life. God did spare Abraham's son, but God did not spare His own Son. He cannot come down from the cross if you are to be saved. And if you are to be saved, you will have to come to the cross. Perhaps that cross is Dothan for you. It is the place of danger and of destiny. If you have never come there, I trust you will come to the Saviour who died for you. It will change your destiny for time and for eternity.

8

KING SOLOMON AND THE
QUEEN OF SHEBA

Solomon

1 Kings 10:24; 2 Chronicles 9:3-4

"And all the earth consulted Solomon, to hear his wisdom, which God had put in his heart" (1 Ki 10:24, NSRB). The more I read this verse the more it impresses me. I am confident that God wants us to pause a moment and look at the significance of it. "All the earth consulted Solomon, to hear his wisdom." You see, God called the people of Israel to be His witnesses, but to be His witnesses in a different way from what He called us to be. You recall that He has called us to go into all the world. Just prior to the day of Pentecost, He told believers to begin at Jerusalem and to go out to Judaea, Samaria, and to the uttermost part of the earth (Ac 1:8). There was to be a moving away from Jerusalem.

Today the witness of the Church is always outward. We must face out if we are to be witnesses for Him. But that was not Israel's case. Israel was never called to go to any nation outside and witness; Israelites were not called to go as missionaries. I have always had great sympathy for Jonah because God asked him to do something that He had not asked His people to do in that day. He asked Jonah to go to Nineveh. That was unusual. This exception to the rule was made because God wanted to save that great city, and He wanted to give them this opportunity. However, the method in that day was this: when the nation Israel was faithful and true to God, worshiping and obeying God in Jerusalem, it would be such a witness to the world that the world would come to Jerusalem, would accept the invitation of Israel, which was, "O come, let us go up to Jerusalem to worship the Lord." The nations of the world would accept that invitation and would come. Did they ever do it? Was the nation Israel ever faithful to God in this respect?

It certainly was.

There was a brief period during the reigns of David and Solomon, which is approximately eighty years, almost a century, in which the word went out. During the reign of Solomon, we are told that all the earth heard, and that is not an exaggerated statement. All the civilized world, every great nation of that day, heard of the wisdom of Solomon, heard of the greatness of Solomon, and came to Jerusalem. Multitudes came to a saving knowledge of God because of that.

Now the incident of the visit of the Queen of Sheba is given to us. She was one of the many who visited Solomon, and her visit is recorded while others are omitted, for very definite reasons, I believe. One reason for its being recorded is that she came farther than anyone else. We are told she came from the ends of the earth, and that means the ends of the civilized world. She came over the only road, the only camel trail that led to Jerusalem; she came from way out yonder. Also her visit was rather unusual because she was a queen and because of the wealth of her kingdom.

The question has always been: from where did she actually come? Two places by the name of Sheba are known to us. One is in Africa and is the country known as Ethiopia. The other is in Asia, and is the little country we know today as Yeman, that little Arabian country which has been left out of the oil situation, and is so poor right

now. Was the Queen of Sheba queen of Yeman or was she
queen of Ethiopia? Bible expositors and scholars are
pretty much divided on this. The queen of Yeman was
known as the queen of the south, and the Lord Jesus Himself, you remember, spoke of the Queen of Sheba as the
queen of the south (Mt 12:42). Also Yeman was known
as the country of spices in the ancient world, and spices
seem to be the noteworthy gift which the Queen of Sheba
brought to Solomon. It is interesting that both countries
have the tradition that in ancient times their queen visited
Solomon. Could there have been another queen who visited Solomon? I have a notion that there could have been
a visit of another which was not recorded, since we are
told that "all the earth consulted Solomon."

The important thing, as far as we are concerned, is that
she came from the uttermost parts of the earth, and she
came to visit this man Solomon.

Now I want you to notice something at this particular
point. Israel was giving a testimony that God said she
should give. At the time of the dedication of the Temple
here is the thing that is said concerning it: "Moreover,
concerning the foreigner, who is not of thy people, Israel,
but is come from a far country for thy great name's sake,
and thy mighty hand, and thy outstretched arm; if they
come and pray in this house, then hear thou from the
heavens, even from thy dwelling place, and do according
to all that the foreigner calleth to thee for, that all people
of the earth may know thy name, and fear thee, as doth thy
people, Israel, and may know that this house, which I have
built, is called by thy name" (2 Ch 6:32-33, NSRB).

This may seem strange to you, but the Temple that
Solomon built was not built for the nation Israel alone. It
was built for the world. It was built that all nations might
come to Jerusalem and worship. One of the saddest
things they did was to make divisions in it. In the days of
the Lord Jesus you find there is a court of the Gentiles;
there's a court for the women, a court for this group and

that group. God never intended that there be this segregation. All were to come to Him on the same plane and basis. This is the thing to which Paul called the attention of his people that made the Church different from the Temple. Speaking of Christ, he said: "For he is our peace, who hath made both one, and hath broken down the middle wall of partition between us, having abolished in his flesh the enmity, even the law of commandments contained in ordinances; for to make in himself of twain one new man, so making peace" (Eph 2:14-15). Christ Jesus broke down the middle wall of partition between Jew and Gentile, between male and female, between rich and poor. All stand together on one plane before Him. Now, my beloved, that is something Israel should have done, that was the purpose of the Temple; that was the reason it was built.

Now I want to turn to another passage of Scripture that records this dedicatory prayer of Solomon's. "Moreover, concerning a foreigner, who is not of thy people, Israel, but cometh out of a far country for thy name's sake (for they shall hear of thy great name, and of thy strong hand, and of thine outstretched arm), when he shall come and pray toward this house, hear thou in heaven, thy dwelling place, and do according to all that the foreigner calleth to thee for, that all people of the earth may know thy name, to fear thee, as do thy people Israel; and that they may know that this house, which I have built, is called by thy name" (1 Ki 8:41-43, NSRB). Solomon is emphasizing, you see, at the dedication of the Temple, that it is a Temple for everyone. It was a place where every person on earth could approach the living and the true God.

That word went out; it went out to the ends of the earth in that day, and it reached the Queen of Sheba. Returning now to the record of the Queen of Sheba's visit, it begins with the words, "And when the queen of Sheba heard." That's all. She first had to hear.

"So then faith cometh by hearing, and hearing by the word of God" (Ro 10:17). The Gospel is something that

you have to hear, and then you have to make your decision
of whether or not you believe God. Faith comes by hearing
the Word of God. This entire incident opens up out yonder
at the ends of the earth with a queen who heard. Then she
acted on what she heard.

My friend, that is the place where God will meet you,
the only place He will meet you. You have to hear. I feel
that my responsibility is to get the Word to that little ear
gate. When I get it to your ear gate, my responsibility is
over. From there on it is your responsibility, and God puts
something between the two ears so you can make a decision relative to Him. The responsibility of every believer
is to get God's Word to the ear gate of our neighbor, and
when we have done that, we have done the thing God has
called us to do.

Now at the time the Queen of Sheba arrived in Jerusalem, it was one of the most interesting cities in the world.
There is not a city on earth today that is as thrilling to
visit as Jerusalem was at that time. The "Graylines" had
a tour that would take you everywhere in that day, and
it would take more than a day to see everything that they
had to show. Jerusalem was very interesting, and was a
tourist attraction.

When this queen arrived, I think she attracted a great
deal of attention; she *had* to be unusual to attract attention. Centuries later wise men came out of the East because a greater than Solomon was there. They came with
the question, "Where is he that is born king of the Jews?"
Jerusalem was troubled. Even old Herod on the throne
was disturbed. By the way, the record does not give us the
number of wise men who came. I think there were three
hundred of them at least, probably more than that. Three
wisemen would never excite Jerusalem; three hundred
would. They had come because *they* had heard.

The Queen of Sheba, I think, excited even more interest
that day when her caravan came inside the walls of Jerusalem. This woman, who comes out of the mysterious

East, is not a wise man, but she is looking for wisdom. She is a queen who has wealth in abundance. You and I today have no notion of the wealth in the Orient of that day. We Americans bury our gold in a cave at Fort Knox, and nobody ever gets to see it. But it was on display in that day. This woman brought wealth with her, and when she arrived, the wealth and luxury of the Orient came inside the walls of Jerusalem. She had an entourage that attracted interest. She had servants and soldiers of every color of skin under the sun. I tell you, the people lined the streets, and no circus has ever attracted the interest that the Queen of Sheba did the day she arrived in Jerusalem.

Now she came with questions. It was the custom in that day for rulers to be asked riddles, what we call today conundrums—tricky, clever questions. Also she had questions that had to do with the heart, questions that related to her eternal destiny because this woman came out of spiritual darkness. Although her court was scintillating and sophisticated, though it was brilliant in many ways, it reflected spiritual darkness.

The record tells us that she was absolutely overwhelmed and overcome by her encounter with King Solomon. First of all, Solomon answered all of her questions. He had answers for every one of them, and, "There was nothing hidden from Solomon which he told her not." In other words, she asked no question that he could not answer. It is said that many of the rulers of Egypt lost face because they were not able to answer questions that were put to them. Solomon never did. Solomon was able to answer all questions.

"And when the queen of Sheba had seen the wisdom of Solomon, and the house that he had built, and the meat of his table, and the sitting of his servants, and the attendance of his ministers, and their apparel; his cupbearers also, and their apparel; and his ascent by which he went up into the house of the LORD, there was no more spirit in her" (2 Ch 9:3-4). Look at this for just a moment. The first thing that impressed her was that he was able to answer all of her questions. The second thing was the tremendous organization and display that he had there. Everywhere she turned, not only pomp and ceremony, but also originality.

How we need originality today. There are too many folk trying to imitate instead of having an impartation of life and translating that in their own way. A very fine young preacher, who was a former student of mine, is having a lot of trouble, I understand. A friend came and talked to me about him because he is tremendously interested in him. He said to me, "Do you know what his trouble is? He's attempting to imitate." And he told me who he is imitating. So I went and talked to this young preacher. I said, "Look, the fellow you're imitating is all right, but you ought to be yourself for the simple reason that you're better as an original than you are as an imitation. In fact, all of us are." God has made each of us an original; let's just be ourselves. How we need originality today!

A fellow came into his office one morning bragging, "Do you know what my wife said to me this morning? She said I was a model husband!" After saying that to several people, finally someone asked him, "Have you ever looked up in the dictionary to see what *model* means?" "No," he said. "Well, you go look it up." So he went to the dictionary and found the meaning to be "a small imitation of the real article." He was a model husband! And, may I say, we have too many small imitations of the real article. We need today that which is original.

Hollywood is dying for the want of genius. They haven't had an original idea in twenty years, and that is the reason smut has become a synonym for sophistication. A great many people do not seem to know the difference, and they go for that dirty, filthy sort of thing, thinking they are being sophisticated. It is just a lack of genius and a lack of ability today.

When the Queen of Sheba came to Jerusalem, I can imagine that she said, "Wow, I have never seen anything like this before! Solomon, you certainly didn't copy anybody!" I'm sure Solomon said, "No, my father David knew God, and God blessed him and revealed these things to him. Now He has blessed me, his son, as I've attempted to carry out the things he wanted done."

Oh, friend, how God wants us today to come to the place where He can use us, and use us in an original way!

Now we are told the third thing which impressed the Queen of Sheba: "His ascent by which he went up into the house of the LORD." *Ascent* is a very unfortunate translation because in the record in 1 Kings (10:5) the Hebrew word is *olah,* meaning "burnt offerings." She was impressed by his burnt offerings which he offered to God. Here in Chronicles the word *ascent* is *aliyyah,* meaning "uppermost place." We are told that in the Temple the king had a private way by which he went up to the altar, but after he got there he was on the same plane as everybody else. That impressed her because down in her country she was far above the level of the crowds. But Solomon, even after he went up his way, stood by that burnt altar just like any other sinner stands before God.

That burnt altar speaks eloquently of the cross of Christ. It is the finest picture of the cross of Christ we have in the Old Testament. That burnt altar was the place where sacrificial animals were burned. These burnt sacrifices, which so impressed her, speak of the person of Christ, of *who* He is; and the sin offering put there speaks of the work of Christ. This woman found, when she came to Jerusalem, that the living and true God was approached only through a sacrifice, a substitute was offered. Even a king had to come as a sinner and stand with the lowest subjects to receive salvation from God. That, I believe, is the way the Queen of Sheba came. The thing that God has revealed is that there is a righteousness which He provides.

I have been recently deeply impressed by this Scripture:

"But now the righteousness of God without the law is manifested, being witnessed by the law and the prophets" (Ro 3:21). You see, the Old Testament pictured this truth in the burnt offering in a way that the Queen of Sheba could understand. All of this was pointing to Christ and a righteousness God was providing for a king or for any sinner that He might accept him into His presence. That righteousness would be through the sacrifice of Another.

"Even the [gift of] righteousness of [from] God which is by faith of Jesus Christ unto all and upon all them that believe: for there is no difference. For all have sinned, and come short of the glory of God" (Ro 3:22-23).

We all stand on the same plane and all must come, and all *can* receive this righteousness. It is my opinion that the Queen of Sheba came to know the living and the true God when she came to Jerusalem. The Lord Jesus, when He was here, said this to the generation around Him: "The queen of the south shall rise up in the judgment with this generation, and shall condemn it: for she came from the farthest parts of the earth to hear the wisdom of Solomon; and, behold, a greater than Solomon is here" (Mt 12:42). As Jesus spoke, the people were turning their backs upon Him, but *she* came from the ends of the earth to learn of Him.

Now what brought her to Jerusalem? As I have said, she heard. But what was it that caused her to act? I suggest several things. First of all, it was her curiosity, I think, that prompted her visit. She kept hearing. Visitors would come to her court with news of Jerusalem. An envoy would report, "We have been to Jerusalem." She'd say, "I've been hearing about Jerusalem. Did you go to the Temple?" They would say, "We sure did. It was a thrilling experience to go into that Temple. We were there on one of their feast days. Wish you could have heard them singing their song. It was tremendous! And there was the altar, and, oh, there was gold, there was silver. It was beautiful. And the service, say, it was wonderful." The

Queen of Sheba would say, "Yes, I've been hearing about that, and I would like to see it for myself. Maybe one of these days I can make the trip." Curiosity.

Now curiosity is something that not only women have—men have it also. If you don't believe it, make an experiment. When I worked on the *Commercial Appeal* in Memphis, there was a columnist who made a bet one day that he could go out on the street and stop traffic by doing nothing in the world but look up. So he got two fellows off the city desk to go with him to the corner of Main and Madison in Memphis. They stepped out there and the three of them looked up. Before long, a half-dozen people had stopped. After they got about twenty there, they slipped out of the crowd and went across the street to watch. For the next thirty minutes traffic was jammed with everybody coming and looking up, and there wasn't a thing to see! Curiosity.

The Queen of Sheba was, I am sure, curious. But there was more than that.

The second thing that motivated the Queen of Sheba was a spirit of inquiry and interest, more than just curiosity. When they told her about an altar where sinners could come—queens could come, kings could come, everybody could come—to receive forgiveness of sins, she had an interest. She said, "I think I'd like to go. I think we'll arrange a trip."

Then there is a third reason. Down deep in her heart there was dissatisfaction and hunger. Here was a queen on a throne. She had everything her little heart wanted. And if there was anything she desired, she got it. Yet there was frustration. She never knew what real satisfaction was. She said to King Solomon: "It was a true report which I heard in mine own land of thine acts, and of thy wisdom: howbeit, I believed not their words, until I came, and mine eyes had seen it: and, behold, the one half of the greatness of thy wisdom was not told me; for thou exceedest the fame that I heard" (2 Ch 9:5-6).

Although she believed in a way, she thought it couldn't

be true, but she believed enough to come. And, my beloved, that is all any sinner needs, just faith enough to come to Christ. Paul said something so important to the Colossians: "For this cause we also, since the day we heard it, do not cease to pray for you, and to desire that ye might be filled with the knowledge of his will in all wisdom and spiritual understanding" (Col 1:9). But, what is "His will"? His Word. That you might be filled with the knowledge of His Word. The Queen of Sheba didn't believe very much, but she came. And when she got there she said, "The half wasn't told me!" Yet she believed enough to come.

My friend, you don't need much faith just to come to Jesus Christ and say, "I'll take You as my Saviour, although I've got a lot of questions, and a lot of problems." Paul prayed that the Colossians might be filled with the knowledge (the *epignosis*, meaning "super-knowledge"). Do you know what kind of knowledge that is? That is the kind of knowledge God gives you. After you have come to Christ, He makes these things real to you.

Faith is not a leap in the dark. It is not just a "hope so." It's not just a betting of your life on God. It is not shutting your eyes and taking a step. Faith rests upon real knowledge. When any man has faith enough just to reach out and take Christ as Saviour, the Spirit of God makes these things *real* to him. I remember when I first came to Him, how little I knew, how little I believed. I've passed that stage now. There are a lot of things I don't even argue about any more. He has made them real to my heart. That to me is the greatest knowledge you can have, to believe Him and then to have Him in turn make these things real to you.

Oh, if you have that dissatisfaction and hunger, just enough to come to Christ and take Him as your Saviour, He will do the rest for you. Paul says in effect, "I'm praying that you might be filled with that super-knowledge of His Word, that these things might be made real to you."

A man wanted to argue with me the other day. He said,

"How do you know the Bible is the Word of God?" I said, "Brother, God has made that thing real to me a thousand different ways. I heard what you've got to say years ago, and I must admit I had doubts then, but God has made His Word so real to me today that it is more real than any of these objections. And God will make it real to you, my friend." This is what Paul is talking about.

The Queen of Sheba came, and I see something else that caused her to come. Self-sacrifice. She came probably 2,000 miles, and in that day they were not running the Super Chief; nor had the super jets been put in operation. When she came, it was a long and arduous trip, which took months of planning. It was a hard dangerous trip, but she undertook it in order to come to Jerusalem.

Today God does not ask you to make a trip anywhere.

"But the righteousness which is of faith speaketh on this wise, Say not in thine heart, Who shall ascend into heaven? (that is, to bring Christ down from above); or, Who shall descend into the deep? (that is, to bring up Christ again from the dead). But what saith it? The word is nigh thee, even in thy mouth, and in thy heart: that is, the word of faith, which we preach; that if thou shalt confess with thy mouth the Lord Jesus, and shalt believe in thine heart that God hath raised him from the dead, thou shalt be saved. For with the heart man believeth unto righteousness; and with the mouth confession is made unto salvation" (Ro 10:6-10).

Today you do not have to make a long trip to Jerusalem. You do not even have to go across the street. He is available to you. You have no excuse. The Queen of Sheba is going to rise up some day and judge America (Mt 12:42). She came 2,000 miles to get saved, but many Americans with the Gospel coming right in to their homes, reject Christ. She will judge them someday. It is close to you today, my friend. You do not have to go anywhere. Sit right where you are and receive Him.

9

THE GREATEST SIN IN ALL
THE WORLD

Hosea

Hosea 1:2

The accusation is often made that the present-day pulpit is weak and uncertain. Furthermore, it is charged that instead of being "a voice in the wilderness," the modern pulpit has settled down comfortably to become a sounding board for the whims and wishes of the multitudes with itching ears. If the charge is true (and it is), it is because the pulpit is reluctant to grapple with the great issues of life. This hesitancy is born of a desire to escape criticism, and it is a dread of becoming offensive to the finer sensibilities. More often it is due to a cowardly fear to face the raw realities of life and to wrestle with the leviathan of living issues. The pulpit quotes poetry and sprinkles rose water.

The theater, movie, monthly magazines, weekly periodicals, daily papers, the radio and television, all deal with life stripped of its niceties. These instruments for reaching and teaching the masses take the gloves off and wade into the problems faced by men daily. As a result, these agencies are more potent and effective in molding the thoughts of folk.

For those who have sat under the shadow of such a pulpit, and for those who have lived such sheltered lives in our churches, the prophecy of Hosea will be shocking and startling. However, we do not want you to be unduly alarmed, for we will not go beyond what is written. For the sake of some timid souls, we shall pull our punches a wee bit. Nevertheless, we are giving this message in the full consciousness that only those who will be offended are those who should be offended. Years ago when I was a boy living in a little town, I recall hearing a country preacher deliver a very homely illustration which was very much to the point. "You know," he said, "when you throw a rock into a bunch of dogs, it is always the hit dog that hollers."

The story behind the prophecy of Hosea is the tragedy of a broken home. The personal experience of Hosea is the background of his message. It concerns the intimate affairs of his home. The home is the rock foundation of society. It is the most important unit in the social structure. It is to society and the state what the atom is to the physical universe. The atom has been called the building block of the universe. The home is just that. It is like the bricks in a building. The color of the individual bricks tell the color of the building. The character of the bricks determine the character of the building. The home is the chain of a nation that runs up and down the streets of every city and hamlet and the highways of the countryside. No chain is stronger than the links which make the chain. Similarly, no nation is stronger than the homes which constitute its total population. The home life of Hosea constitutes the background of his message to the nation of Israel.

The home is where we live, move, and have our being. It is in the home that we are ourselves. We dress physically and psychologically to go out, but within the walls of the place called home, we remove our masks.

Because of the strategic position of the home, God has thrown about the home certain safeguards to protect it. God has surrounded the home with a wall of instruction due to its importance. He has moved into the home to direct its intimate relationships. Marriage, which is the backbone of the home, has received more attention from God than any other institution.

Society never made marriage; it found it. God made marriage. It was His gift to mankind. Marriage rests upon His direct Word, "What, therefore, God hath joined together, let not man put asunder." God performed the first marriage ceremony. He gave the first bride away. He blessed the first couple. Marriage is more than a legal contract, more than an economic cornerstone of a nation, more than the union of mutual love; it is an act of God. It rests upon His command. Many young people think that all they need in order to get married is a license and a preacher. They need God. If He does not bless the union, it is not marriage.

God has given a drive to the race to reproduce within the framework of marriage: "The twain shall be one flesh," and "Be fruitful and multiply." Marriage is a sacred relationship, and it is a holy union. Paul said, "He sinneth not; let them marry." The New Testament sums up the mind of God, "Marriage is honorable in all" (Heb 13:4). Therefore, marriage cannot be broken by a legal act, a fit of temper, or self-will. There are only two acts which break marriage (real marriage, that is):

1. The first act which breaks marriage is the death of either the man or woman. "For the woman which hath an husband is bound by the law to her husband so long as he liveth; but if the husband be dead, she is loosed from the law of her husband" (Ro 7:2). This is accepted by all Christians as a legitimate breaking of the marriage relationship.

2. Unfaithfulness on the part of either the man or woman breaks asunder the marriage relationship. This rips the relationship in two and drives a wedge into that which has been made one. Under the Mosaic system, a man or woman who was guilty of adultery was dealt with

summarily. Such perfidy merited death, and it was
meted out without mercy. Listen to the Law:

"And the man that committeth adultery with another
man's wife, even he that committeth adultery with his
neighbor's wife, the adulterer and the adulteress shall
surely be put to death" (Lev 20:10). "But if this thing be
true, and the tokens of virginity be not found for the
damsel: then they shall bring out the damsel to the door
of her father's house, and the men of her city shall stone
her with stones that she die: because she hath wrought
folly in Israel, to play the whore in her father's house: so
shalt thou put evil away from among you" (Deu 22:20-21).

Some zealous Christians use Romans 7:2 as the basis
for the extreme viewpoint that a divorced person who has
a living mate can never remarry. They forget that under
the Law the married person who was guilty of fornication
was stoned to death and the innocent party, under the Law,
did not have a living partner. The guilty person was some-
where under a pile of stones. (Southern California would
be covered with rock piles were the Mosaic law enforced
today!)

Another item concerning the Law which needs amplifi-
cation is the reference in Deuteronomy which seems to pre-
clude the man from any charge of guilt. The facts are that
the analogy is to Christ and the Church. He is never under
suspicion: the Church is. It is true that the Law uses the
masculine gender oftentimes when it means either man or
woman. The word is used as a generic term; for instance,
mankind means both men and women. Even today a legal
document reads, "The party of the first part . . . if *he*,"
when the party of the first part may be *she*.

In spite of this explanation, there is a sense in which the
Bible teaches a double standard. This does not mean there
is a high standard for women and a low standard for men,
but it does mean that they are different. This is an estab-

lished custom in our modern society. Every department store has a women's department and a men's department. Every hospital has a women's ward and a men's ward. This line of demarcation is recognized on every level of the social world. I believe that this is a valid distinction. For this same reason, I take my watch to one repairman and my car to another. The watch is a more delicate mechanism and needs the attention of a different mechanic with a different technique.

Woman is made finer than man. It is more tragic when she goes wrong than when a man does. It is not that sin in one is worse than in another, but the results are far more detrimental. In my limited ministry, I have seen children overcome the handicap of a ne'er-do-well father, but I have never seen children turn out right with a bad mother. A sorry father is a serious handicap for a child, but a good mother more than compensates. Mother is the center of the home. A godly mother said some time ago when she refused to accept an office in a church organization, "I am a missionary to the nursery, and there are three pairs of eyes watching me. I want to direct them to God."

The prophecy of Hosea must be contrasted with God's ideal of marriage and of womanhood. God's revelation of marriage and His controls for it, must be written in letters of light over the sordid story of Hosea's experience. This is the correct method. Recently, our freeway markers were changed and enlarged. Instead of black letters on a white background, now the signs are white letters on a black background. This is scriptural. God writes His revelation and salvation on the black background of man's sin. God's high standard must be written over Hosea's home; only then will we catch the message.

Now we are prepared to examine the story behind the headlines in Hosea. In the hill country of Ephraim, in one of the many little towns not on the maps of the world, lived two young people. One was a boy by the name of Hosea, the other was a girl by the name of Gomer. They fell in

love. It is the same story which has been repeated millions
of times, but it never grows old. Apparently, they fell
madly in love. Then the girl went bad for some unaccount-
able reason. To suggest any explanation is to speculate.
She even resorted to what is referred to as the "oldest profession known to man." Hosea was brokenhearted, and
shame filled his soul. He must have thought about his
recourse to the Mosaic law. He could have brought her
before the elders of the town and demanded the Law be
enforced. In that case she would have been stoned, for she
had betrayed him. He would have been justified.

Does this not remind you of another story which oc-
curred in these same hills seven hundred years later? Another young man by the name of Joseph was engaged to a
young lady named Mary. He thought of putting her away
privately instead of publicly stoning her. But Mary was
innocent of any wrongdoing. Gomer was not. She was
guilty and so labeled. There was no question of Gomer's
guilt as far as the record is concerned.

The book of Hosea opens at this juncture of the story. It
opens with the most startling and shocking statement in
the entire Bible. "The beginning of the word of the LORD
by Hosea. And the LORD said to Hosea, Go, take unto thee
a wife of whoredoms and children of whoredoms; for the
land hath committed great whoredom, departing from the
LORD" (Ho 1:2).

Some have not been willing to concede this as the actual
experience of the prophet and have dismissed this strong
language by calling it an allegory. Such trifling with the
Word of God waters it down to a harmless solution which
is more sickening than stimulating. Let's face it: God commanded Hosea to break the Mosaic law. The Law said to
stone her, but God said to marry her. The thing God commanded Hosea to do must have caused him to revolt in
every fiber of his being. Where would God find a man
today who would go that far with Him?

Hosea did not demur; he obeyed explicitly. He took

Gomer in holy wedlock, and he gave her his name. She came into his home as his wife. Listen to the apostle: "What? know ye not that he which is joined to an harlot is one body? for two, saith he, shall be one flesh" (1 Co 6:16).

You may be sure that the tempo of gossip was stepped up in their home town. Someone has said that God made the country, and man made the city, but the devil made the little town. The gossip of folk in a little town is cruel and brutal, although they don't mean it to be. The mistake of an individual is known by all and forgotten by none. Hosea's home became a desert island in a sea of criticism. It was the isolation ward in local society. A case of leprosy in the home would not have broken off contact with the outside world more effectively. Poor Hosea!

Children were born in this home. There were three— two boys and one girl. Their names, in their meanings, tell the awful story. And there is the larger meaning and message for the nation Israel.

Jezreel was the oldest. His name means "God will scatter." The reference is directly to an evil event in the life of the Northern Kingdom. Jehu killed the children of Ahab and Jezebel. Although God commanded it, Jehu did it in self-will and hatred. God judged the house of Ahab but avenged that judgment on the house of Jehu for its brutality and lack of pity. There was no repentance. God will scatter Israel, but there will be mercy in His judgment.

The second child was Lo-ruhamah which means that she never knew a father's pity. It was not that she was an orphan, but because she was not sure who her father was. What a scandal in the home of Hosea! That generation of Israel would not know the pity of God, but God would remember to be gracious to later generations.

The last child was Lo-ammi, which means "not my people." There is something very insinuating here which I feel should be mentioned. If you put this in the singular, it would mean "not my child." Hosea here is frankly revealing the scandal of his home. His experience pictured the people of Israel who were, as the Lord Jesus Christ said of the religious rulers of His day, of their father, the devil. They were no longer the legitimate children of God. However, God would not throw over the nation. These three children tell the sad story of Hosea, and in the larger sphere, the declension of the Northern Kingdom, which is called Ephraim in this book.

This does not end the record. Gomer ran away from home. She returned to her former profession. She became a common prostitute. You would think that God would permit Hosea to give her up now. Not so! God sent Hosea to bring her back. She refused, and he sent the children to plead with their mother. She continued to refuse. As women of this sort did in those days, she sold herself into slavery. Hosea bought her and brought her back by force. It would indeed be gratifying to be able to say that she became a good wife and mother. Perhaps she did. Certainly by inference that is the conclusion that I draw, since the analogy is to Israel, and finally God will triumph with the nation. The victory of love is the theme of the book.

This concludes the personal story of Hosea. It is a sordid and sorry account of his domestic affairs. For the sake of poetic justice, we perhaps should say that Hosea saved his home. This, however, is not the purpose of recording his experience. God was disciplining this man to speak for Him to a nation that was guilty of spiritual adultery. Out of a home scarred by shame, this man stepped before the nation with a message of fire. He stood before a nation with a heartbreak that was intolerable, with scalding tears coursing down his saddened cheeks, an ache of soul, and a shame of spirit, to denounce a people who were guilty of religious harlotry. He walked out of a home broken by sin and scandal, a home saddened, soiled, and sullied by the ugliness of sin.

He denounced the nation and declared a verdict of guilty for the crime of crimes. He said simply, but specifi-

cally, that sin is as black as can be, that God will punish
sin wherever He finds it, but that God loves the sinner.
When a nation acknowledges God, turns to Him, is blessed
of Him, and experiences His love, then subsequently turns
from God to idols, that sin is labeled harlotry.

God took Israel out of Egypt. He led them through the
wilderness, and His own explanation was, "Ye have seen
what I did unto the Egyptians, and how I bore you on
eagles' wings, and brought you unto myself" (Ex 19:4).

This people made a golden calf and turned to it from
God. God brought them back to Himself. At the division
of the kingdom, they made two calves, and again God attempted to woo them back to Himself. The charge made
repeatedly against them was that they went a whoring
after other gods. Candidly stated, the charge was that
Israel was playing the harlot. This is sin at its worst. Let
us not misunderstand. We are not suggesting the sensa-
tional idea that the seventh commandment is written in
neon lights, and breaking it is the chief sin.

We are now ready to ask the question and to answer it:
"What is the greatest sin in all the world?" Two have been
suggested by others as the greatest:

1. Unbelief. It is true that there is no remedy for unbelief. God has a remedy for all sin, but unbelief means
   to reject the remedy. Nevertheless, multitudes are in
   unbelief because they have never heard the Gospel.
   When they hear, they will believe. Others have honest
   doubts. The honest doubter is a rare specimen, but
   there are a few. If a man has an honest doubt, "he will
   beat his music out." Unbelief is not the greatest sin.
2. Sin against light. This is coming close but it misses the
   mark. Surely Israel had light, and light does add to the
   exceeding sinfulness of sin. In one sense, sin is sin, and
   it is infinite since it is against God. In the economy of
   God, it is difficult to say that there is a sin that is worse

than any other when God says, "For whosoever shall keep the whole law, and yet offend in one point, he is guilty of all" (Ja 2:10).

The individual or nation that is guilty of sin makes the difference. If a man or a nation has had the light of God and then rejects it, that makes their sin worse. The sin of Los Angeles is worse than the sin of Moscow. I would rather be a Hottentot in the darkness of an African jungle, bowing down in fear before an idol of a witch doctor, than to be a cynic who sits within the sound of the Gospel in any Bible-believing church from Sunday to Sunday and continues on without responding to God's invitation and receiving the light of heaven. Yes, sin against light is heinous. There is, however, a sin that is even greater.

3. Sin against love. This is sin at its worst. This is the greatest sin in all the world. This is the revelation of Hosea. Gomer was not only guilty of breaking the marriage vow, but she sinned against one who loved her. That is unspeakable. That is worse than the animism and animalism of the heathen world. It is deeper and darker than the immorality of the underworld and the demonism of the overworld. Hosea knew what sin was; he knew what love was. Sin against love aggravates sin. Israel knew the love of God. She knew His deliverance, His redemption, His protection, His forgiveness, His revelation, and His love. Israel turned to dumb idols and gave herself to them. This was sin against love, and nothing was worse. God would not give her up; love will triumph. The story is told in three verses in Hosea.

Here is the charge: "Ephraim is joined to idols: let him alone" (Ho 4:17).

Here is the pulsating passion of an infinite God. "How shall I give thee up, Ephraim? how shall I deliver thee,

Israel? how shall I make thee as Admah? how shall I set
thee as Zeboim? mine heart is turned within me, my re-
pentings are kindled together" (Ho 11:8).

Here is the victory. "Ephraim shall say, What have I
to do any more with idols? I have heard him, and ob-
served him: I am like a green fir tree. From me is thy fruit
found" (Ho 14:8).

There will come a day when Israel will turn from idols
back to God. (This is my reason for believing that Gomer
became a faithful wife.)

When a young couple have made shipwreck of their marriage and come to me, my first inquiry concerns their personal relationship. Recently in the Bay area, a young
couple came to me with their problem. I asked them if
they still loved each other. Tears filled their eyes, and
they confesed eagerly that they did. It is unnecessary to
say that they are working out their problem. When love
is gone, it looks hopeless; but with love there is hope.

Does this shocking description of spiritual adultery fit
the Church? The Church is described as the bride of
Christ. "I have espoused you . . . that I may present you
as a chaste virgin to Christ" (2 Co 11:2). To the Ephesian
church John wrote, "I have somewhat against thee, because thou hast left thy first love" (Rev 2:4). It is also
interesting to note that *Hosea* means "salvation" and is
another form of *Joshua*. *Joshua* (lit., *Yeshua*) is the Hebrew of the Greek form *Jesus*. The Church is the Bride of
the New Testament Hosea, but has the Bride played the
harlot?

The harlotry of worldliness has saturated the Church.
Even conservative circles have not escaped. Every device
is used to attract the crowd and please the mob. The
Church has attempted to be up to date in its methods without actually letting the world in. At present, the distinction is erased and the flood of worldly devices has filled
the Church. Hosea called this spiritual adultery. We call

it a sincere attempt to reach the unsaved and dismiss it as nothing. In fact, it shocks us no longer. As a result, the church has lost its influence. On any given Sunday we are told that 80 percent of the population of Southern California have not been inside any church.

Let us be very personal. What is your personal relationship with Christ? Has a cloud come between? Has some sin eclipsed His presence? Are you indifferent? Are you trying to compensate by criticizing or turning to some feverish service? Before the Lord Jesus put Simon Peter in harness, He asked the heart-searching question, "Lovest thou me?" This is just as poignant and pertinent now as it was that early dawn by the Sea of Galilee.

McCheyne and Rutherford, as well as a host of others, cried out to God in an agony of soul. As you listen to them, you might get the impression that they had committed the unpardonable sin. What was the deadly grievance in their hearts? Listen to them, for they are confessing their indifference and coldness. Friend, if *they* were tepid, *we* are in deep freeze. When a person is freezing, we are told, he lapses into indifference before the coming of unconsciousness and death. May God alert us before we freeze to death! May we be given grace to detect our coldness. Spurgeon stopped one day in the middle of a busy street in London in the attitude of prayer. A friend of long standing who saw him asked what he was doing. He replied, "A cloud suddenly came between my Saviour and my soul. I stopped to confess my sin and remove the cloud." Would to God we were as sensitive to sin and conscious of our relationship to Christ.

If you are a person who has not yet turned to Christ as Saviour, do not take comfort in this message. You are not yet a Christian, but you have heard of the love of God. It is simply stated in John 3:16: "For God so loved the world, that he gave his only begotten Son, that whosoever believeth in him should not perish, but have everlasting life."

You have turned your back on the greatest display of love in the universe—the cross of Christ. The explanation is found in these words, "He loved me [you] and He gave Himself for me [you]." Do not be indifferent to such love. Do not reject it. The Saviour loves you and will receive you.

> When I survey the wondrous cross,
>   On which the Prince of glory died,
> My richest gain I count but loss,
>   And pour contempt on all my pride.
>
> Were the whole realm of nature mine,
>   That were a present far too small;
> Love so amazing, so divine,
>   Demands my soul, my life, my all.

                                        ISAAC WATTS